GEM MINERALS OF IDAHO

D1303193

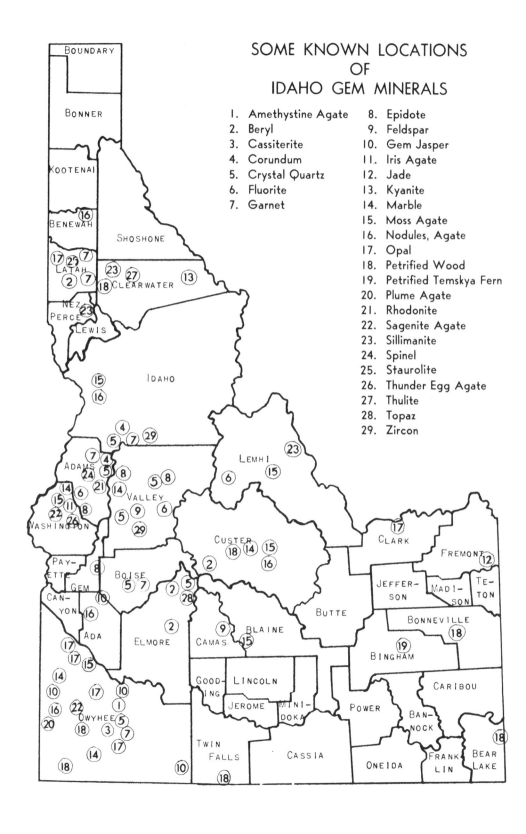

SOME KNOWN LOCATIONS
OF
IDAHO GEM MINERALS

1. Amethystine Agate
2. Beryl
3. Cassiterite
4. Corundum
5. Crystal Quartz
6. Fluorite
7. Garnet
8. Epidote
9. Feldspar
10. Gem Jasper
11. Iris Agate
12. Jade
13. Kyanite
14. Marble
15. Moss Agate
16. Nodules, Agate
17. Opal
18. Petrified Wood
19. Petrified Temskya Fern
20. Plume Agate
21. Rhodonite
22. Sagenite Agate
23. Sillimanite
24. Spinel
25. Staurolite
26. Thunder Egg Agate
27. Thulite
28. Topaz
29. Zircon

GEM MINERALS
OF IDAHO

By

JOHN A. BECKWITH

DRAWINGS AND MAPS BY JANE BECKWITH

CAXTON PRESS
Caldwell, Idaho
2007

First printing August, 1972
Second printing March, 1974
Third printing January, 1977
Fourth printing July, 1980
Fifth printing August, 1987
Sixth printing May, 1994
Seventh printing September, 1998
Eighth printing September, 2003
Ninth printing October, 2007

International Standard Book Number 978-0-87004-228-7

Library of Congress Catalog No. 70-150817

Printed and bound in the United States of America by
The CAXTON PRESS
Caldwell, Idaho 83605
175543

"To my wife, Mildred, whose encouragement, companionship on field trips, and many hours of hard work on the manuscript made completion of this book possible."

JOHN A. BECKWITH

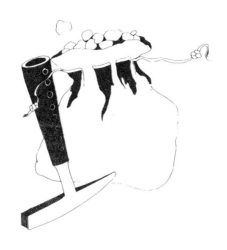

TABLE OF CONTENTS

LIST OF ILLUSTRATIONS

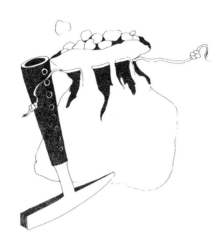

LIST OF MAPS

PREFATORY NOTE

THIS BOOK is not a textbook in mineralogy. Its appeal, we hope, will be to that large number of readers who have only a popular interest in the special field of gem minerals. Scientific terminology has been avoided so far as it was possible to do so without loss of accuracy. No attempt has been made to include a description of all the gem minerals that occur in Idaho nor of all the sources of gem minerals.

Facts have been drawn from many sources, especially reports from many rockhound friends. A lifetime of living and rock hunting in Idaho has permitted personal authentication of many of these facts. Those unauthenticated the reader can readily accept as true, since rockhounds are never carried away by their enthusiasm and their accounts of sources and the quality of material discovered are always accurate.

GEM MINERALS OF IDAHO

INTRODUCTION

MAN'S INTEREST in gems is far older than his interest in clothes. From the earliest times he has sought gem minerals suitable for personal adornment and ornamentation. Shiny pebbles in the streams attracted him. Glittering crystals in outcrops arrested his attention. The rainbow hues of surface minerals fascinated him. The radiant luster of pearls and the beauty of coral he discovered in his search for food.

In addition to satisfying man's desire to possess these beautiful objects for aesthetic reasons only, they became emblematic of the virtues, symbols of good fortune, safety, security, omens of good and sometimes bad luck. Some of these age-old superstitions we still associate with certain gemstones, particularly birthstones.

Man's search for gems has been continuous and unrelenting, but in the last few decades the search has become much intensified. Never before has interest in gemology been so high as it is today. This may be accounted for partly because people now have more leisure time. Undoubtedly a far more important reason, however, is the discovery and manufacture of effective abrasives and the increased production of industrial diamonds, all now within the financial reach of the man with an average income.

This growth of interest is widespread. People of either sex, all ages, and all walks of life have become eager adherents. In areas such as Idaho where gem minerals are plentiful, the growth and spread of the interest in exploration and processing of gem minerals has been particularly remarkable.

Gem minerals are the by-products of such vast geological processes as volcanic action, seeping of mineral-laden waters over eons of time, the violent erosive action of moving ice masses and surging new streams, and the convulsions and tremendous pressures of gigantic rock masses being uplifted and formed into mountains.

It takes but a brief kaleidoscopic review to reveal that hardly any other section of the world has experienced more gem mineral-forming forces than Idaho. In the north are the alluvial and glacial deposits of the lake country and the metamorphic schists of the Belt Series. Along the central western border the mineral-rich basalts and andesites of the Hells Canyon region rise from the depths of the grand canyon of the Snake to the majestic heights of the Seven Devils Peaks. The black, jagged basalt of ancient lava flows spreads over much of the Snake River Plains of southern Idaho. In southeastern Idaho are the phosphate beds, limestones, and sediments of waters that covered the area in the geological past. Rugged cliffs of pink and purple rhyolite intermixed with the cream-colored Payette formation lake beds color the canyons and high plateaus of the Owyhee desert. All these areas hold rewards for the gem hunter, but the area of greatest interest is the thousands of square miles of gray-green or blue granite covering the whole central area of the State and known as the Idaho batholith. This is a primitive area of soaring mountain peaks, a land grooved by canyons of profound depth and grandeur cut by rushing mountain streams. The gem mineral possibilities of this vast area are practically unexplored.

These vast dramas of the geologic past produced gems that are still waiting, after the passing of tens of thousands of years, for discovery by man. Myriad stream beds and canyon

Courtesy Idaho Department of Commerce and Development
Gems of rare beauty can be found in the gravel beds of myriad streams

walls, countless mountain slopes and high plateaus, have gems of rare beauty and quality to reward the gem hunter for his search. Idaho is truly a gem hunter's paradise.

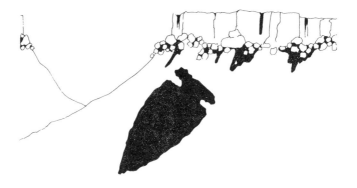

CRYSTALLINE QUARTZ

OF ALL THE minerals, quartz occurs most frequently and in a greater variety of forms and ways. It touches the daily life of everyone. In electronics it is used as a frequency standard. When fused it is used in the manufacture of optical instruments, eye glasses, and laboratory vessels. Quartz sand also has many uses, such as the manufacture of glass, porcelain, sandpaper, and scouring soap. As dust it takes the polish off many of our finished gemstones.

Gem mineral quartz occurs in almost every country, and the use of all its varieties as gem material has been known since the most ancient times. Today it is the most commonly used gem mineral, particularly if glass is included. The varieties of quartz include more than half the precious and semi-precious stones. In addition, from quartz are fashioned many such articles of art as vases, goblets, spheres, and figurines.

Because varieties of crystalline quartz may vary slightly from varieties of chalcedony in physical and optical properties, many mineralogists classify them, and so treat them, as different species. Further, the chalcedonies always occure in cryptocrystalline, massive form—that is, as aggregates in which the individual crystal grains are not readily detected. On the other hand, crystalline varieties always occur in crystal form or as a homogeneous mass not composed of crystal grains. Because of these facts and for clarity of presentation, the crystalline and chalcedony varieties of quartz are treated separately.

Clear, colorless crystalline quartz is known as rock crystal. Its occurrence in excellent quality is widespread and abundant. Crystals may be so small that they may be seen only with the aid of a microscope or immense ones weighing as much as five hundred pounds. It was to rock crystal that the Greeks first gave the name *crystal* meaning *ice*. They concluded the clear crystals to be ice frozen so hard it would never melt.

People of many nations have believed that the future can be foretold by gazing into a sphere of rock crystal. This belief that a spirit dwells within the crystal ball and will reveal the fate of the seeker is older than recorded history.

Gem stones cut brilliant from rock crystals are properly known as rhinestones. However, because this term has been debased by using it to designate any colorless foil back, cut or molded brilliant, genuine quartz brilliants are now commonly designated as "diamonds" with a locality prefix—that is, Arkansas diamonds, Arizona diamonds, Herkimer diamonds.

Rock crystal that displays an iridescence by interference of light from air-filled cracks is known as iris or rainbow quartz crystal.

Because quartz is the last mineral to crystalize from a magma, it frequently includes crystals of many other minerals. Rock crystals containing long, needle-like crystals of rutile, tourmaline, or actinolite are called rutilated quartz. If the included crystals in a finished stone are fine and heavy, it is designated as a Venus Hair or Thetis Hair Stone.

Rock crystal is frequently dyed by crackling the material and saturating the cracks with artificial coloring. Pleasing colors of all hues result. Such dying is easily detected because the color is unevenly distributed and generally too vivid to be true.

Because large pieces of flawless rock crystal are easily obtained, the value of a particular object depends upon the qual-

Quartz crystals

ity of the workmanship, including polishing, cutting, and carving, that is reflected in the finished product.

The violet to red-purple variety of crystalline quartz is amethyst. It is frequently flawed and feathered and of a light tone or uneven coloring, all of which reduce its value. Heating or burning sometimes improves the evenness of the color, but a colorless or brownish-yellow topaz quartz is just as likely to result from this process. A skilled lapidary can improve poor coloring by proper orientation and cutting. Deep purplish-red to purple-red hues with the usual metallic brilliancy of amethyst are most esteemed—the deeper violets even more so, as they hold their color better in artificial light.

The amethyst offers the greatest amount of beauty for the least money of any of the better known gems. Recent discoveries of large quantities of amethyst of good quality have tended to reduce the overall value of the material, but finished gems of fine, even, dark color tones are in demand and command high prices.

The word *amethyst* comes from Greek and means "not to intoxicate." The Greeks once superstitiously believed that wine drunk from an amethystine goblet would prevent the intoxication of the drinker, no matter the amount of wine consumed. Amethyst is also generally recognized as the birthstone of February and as such, if worn by people born in that month, averts evil and brings good fortune. The gem is also considered sacred and is often used for bishops' rings, originally cut as intaglio for use as a signet. Amethyst is the gem in the Pope's ring of authority, and an amethyst ring is given to cardinals upon their investiture. The stone has generally been considered to protect its wearer from bodily harm in battle. For this reason many Crusaders wore an amethyst attached to a rosary.

Crystalline quartz in colors from yellow to red-orange to orange-brown is citrine, sometimes called topaz quartz. Yellow citrine quartz, which is tougher, cheaper, and usually freer from flaws than topaz, is frequently sold as topaz. This is particularly true for stones used in men's rings where the velvety body appearance is not so desired as toughness, a necessary attribute. The dark burnt orange or Madeira citrine facets into beautiful and valuable stones.

Smoky, grayish, brown, or black crystalline quartz is generally known in the field simply as smoky quartz. A finished stone, however, is nearly always designated as a cairngorm or, sometimes, Scotch topaz. Cairngorm is the name of a mountain in Scotland, where smoky quartz is found in abundance. It also occurs generally in the granites of Scotland and is found as water-worn pebbles in most of the streams. The gem is much used to decorate the weapons and clothes of Highlanders and is regarded as the national gem of Scotland. Strong heating of some pale amethyst crystals produces yellowish, brownish, or reddish citrine material. Stones cut from such material are known as burnt topaz. Cairngorm of a rich brown color is most desirable; however, very dark or black is also popular.

Quartz colored pink, rose-red, and pale rose is rose quartz. Although it is distinctly a variety of crystalline quartz, its occurrence is usually massive with crystals rarely large enough to be seen by the unaided eye. The principal use of this material is for beads, novelties, and ornamental objects. Like amethyst, it is sometimes carved. The deeper shades are the most valuable. All tones tend to fade in sunlight or when the material is heated. Occasional specimens of rose quartz, cut as a sphere, exhibit a bright star in transmitted light. Fashioned as cabs with a foil back, they make very satisfactory starred gems.

A rare variety of crystalline quartz, indigo blue and translucent, is siderite or sapphire quartz. Another deep blue variety but much more common in occurrence is dumortierite quartz, colored by the mineral dumortierite. It is opaque and, like rose quartz, always occurs in massive form. This blue variety closely resembles lapis-lazuli and is sometimes improperly sold as such.

The crystalline quartz variety aventurine usually occurs in a bright green color; however, it is sometimes grayish, yellowish, or brownish. Aventurine exhibits a characteristic sheen known as aventurescence. The color depends upon the inclusion causing the phenomenon. Inclusions of fushsite produce a greenish adventurescence; mica, silvery, brassy or golden; hematite and goethite, reddish.

Tiger-eye is usually classified as a variety of crystalline quartz, even though in crystal structure it is a pseudomorph. The crystal structure of blue asbestos has been completely replaced by quartz. It is yellow, brown, blue, or red and always opaque and has a silky, fibrous body appearance when polished flat. Cut in cabochon it exhibits a chatoyancy of distinct moving bands of light, occasionally narrow enough and defined distinctly enough to be classified as cat's-eye.

Common crystalline quartz, translucent to opaque and white to gray, frequently referred to as milky quartz or by miners as bull quartz, seldom occurs in gem quality. Occasional pieces will display a narrow band of light when cut cabochon and finished stones from this material are known as quartz cat's-eyes or occidental cat's-eyes. Some cabochons containing attractive patterns of free gold are also cut from this material.

Quartzite, the last of the crystalline quartz varieties sometimes used for gem fashioning, is a metamorphic sandstone. Sometimes it is so hard and resistant, as a result of heat and pressure in the metamorphic processes, that it will break as easily across the grains as around them. Consequently, it takes and retains a good polish and if the color and pattern are attractive, makes a satisfactory gem material.

Common massive quartz occurs throughout Idaho in veins and as masses in rocks of all kinds. Sometimes the occurrence is in connection with metal-bearing veins, but frequently it occurs in large deposits which do not contain any other mineral. It varies from milky white to bluish or gray. Similar massive quartz occurs in pegmatites and as grains in granites and other igneous rocks. When these rocks disintegrate, the quartz, being chemically the most stable constituent, remains behind in the form of waterworn grains. Much of the sand of Idaho is made of such grains. Consolidation of this sand gives rise to extensive formations of sandstone in the State. Some of the sandstone is changed by metamorphism to quartzite. Like massive quartz, most quartzite has little gem significance, but occasional pieces having attractive color or pattern are fashioned.

Crystalline quartz of gem value occurs in abundance in all parts of Idaho. Vugs in ore bodies, granites, and lavas are lined with beautiful quartz crystals. Because quartz is associated with the occurrence of practically every other mineral, many specimens of gem quality are recovered incidental to the search for other gem minerals. The working of mine dumps, placer tailings, and gravel bars of streams yields satisfying results.

Some particular areas of the State are of interest to the individual who is specifically hunting for crystalline quartz of gem quality.

Rock crystal and smoky quartz is plentiful in the placer workings of Rocky Flat in Adams County both as rolled pebbles or small crystals. The material is of excellent quality (see Field Trip 2).

In Blaine County, and especially on Pole Creek, a tributary of the Salmon River, chalcedony geodes weathered from basalts of the area are lined with beautifully colored, sharp amethyst crystals.

The mine dumps, placer workings, and gravel bars of the Idaho City area of Boise County contain much desirable material, particularly the mine dumps in the Quartzburg district. The Gold Hill Mine dump has proven to be especially rewarding.

In Custer County at the head of Wildhorse Canyon at the eastern base of Hyndman Peak, quartz crystals, clear, transparent, and beautifully perfect, line hollow veins in the quartzite and gneiss. At many places in the upper Lost River Valley clear quartz crystals line chalcedony geodes weathered from the lavas. Some of these geodes are a foot in diameter and the crystals are correspondingly larger. Geodes from the Antelope Creek and Road Creek areas near Arco contain similar clear crystals; however, an occasional geode is lined with amethyst crystals.

The placer tailings at Featherville and Rocky Bar in Elmore County are rich in crystalline quartz gem material. In the Dismal Swamp area northwest of Rocky Bar, smoky quartz crystals of exceedingly fine gem quality occur. A few of these crystals are over a foot in length and four to six inches in diameter. Stones cut from this material have an attractive rich brown color (see Field Trip 4).

Clear and smoky quartz crystals, crystal fragments, and rolled pebbles of gem desirability occur in the placer tailings of Ruby Meadows in Idaho County. Although the specimens there are not plentiful, careful searching usually results in satisfying finds. (see Field Trip 2).

Crystalline quartz material occurs throughout Owyhee County, especially lining geodes found in its western parts. The mine dumps of the DeLamar-Silver City area are highly productive. Numerous vugs in the ore bodies are lined with beautiful clear and amethyst crystals. Clusters of these crystals excavated during the mining process were subsequently discarded upon the dumps. Crystal clusters and individual crystals eroded free are scattered on the hillsides around Silver City. One of the best hunting areas is Long Gulch, three-quarters of a mile south of Silver City (see Field Trip 10).

Clear rock crystal, some beautifully rutilated, has been recovered from a crystal location northwest of Donnelly in Valley County. The placer tailings at Paddy Flat and Big Creek near Cascade contain smoky quartz and amethyst material. The small mountain just north of Cascade continues to produce quartz crystals. The smoky quartz is particularly fine and yields cut cairngorms of superb quality (see Field Trip 3).

Small but desirable clear and amethyst crystals line geodes occurring at the Beacon Hill and Hog Creek areas north of Weiser in Washington County (see Field Trip 5).

For the individual whose interest is crystalline gem material, Idaho is indeed a happy hunting ground.

Photographed by W. M. Beckert

Smoky quartz crystals from Dismal Swamp

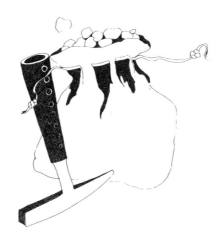

CHALCEDONY QUARTZ

CHALCEDONY AND crystalline quartz have the same chemical composition, although chalcedony usually has greater amounts of impurities. While crystalline quartz is generally a primary deposit, chalcedony is usually a secondary deposit, filling seams, fissures, veins, and cavities in the rock. Further, because chalcedony always occurs in massive cryptocrystalline forms and usually has slightly lower physical and optical properties, it is generally regarded as a separate mineral species.

The identity of the multiude of tiny, imperfectly shaped crystals making up a piece of chalcedony can usually be revealed only under X-ray examination. However, the fact that it is so made up is important to gemologists because it means the material is more or less porous and can be stained or dyed.

The varieties of chalcedony can be properly designated simply as chalcedony with a color prefix—that is, blue chalcedony, green chalcedony, black chalcedony, etc. Several more complex classifications are in common use and generally accepted. However, because chalcedony occurs in such a wide range of deposits and forms, many areas have an involved and detailed

Courtesy United States Bureau of Land Management
Juniper Mountain Plateau, Owyhee County

classification and terminology understandable only locally. In the following discussion of chalcedony varieties, only the more generally accepted and understood classifications are used.

First, it should be recognized that agate is not a variety of chalcedony. Accurately used, the term applies to chalcedony having definite colors, patterns, layers, bands, scenes, or markings. Among gemologists it is used popularly to designate any chalcedony suitable for gem cutting.

White, gray, brown, and pale grayish-blue kinds, of massive cryptocrystalline varieties of quartz are usually referred to simply as chalcedony. Some translucent white specimens, however, will display a moving light when cut cabochon. These are known as chalcedony moonstones and in their finer qualities as oriental moonstones.

Apple-green or pale, yellowish-green chalcedony is chrysoprase. Frequently this material is cracked and has brown marks. Further, it fades in sunlight and heat tends to discolor it. Other material can be artificially colored, but it seldom obtains the fine light green color quality of the natural material. In its finest qualities chrysoprase is rare and valuable. Translucent material of good color is sometimes mounted with diamonds in platinum.

Chalcedony frequently includes crystals of such minerals as rutile, hornblende, tourmaline, actinolite, calcium, magnesium, or manganese. Translucent to semi-transparent chalcedony having tree-like inclusions is dendrite agate. If the inclusions resemble moss, the material is moss agate. A few authorities restrict this classification to green inclusions only, and call those having brownish or grayish inclusions mocha stone. If the inclusions suggest a plume, usually white or black, the material is plume agate. If the inclusions suggest a landscape scene, the material is landscape or picture agate. Finally, if the inclusions are needle-like, the material is sagenite agate. If the fibers are tangled and hair-like, the material is further classified as Venus hair agate. The value of these types of agate depends very much upon the attractiveness of the pattern of the inclusions and the skill of fashioning.

Dark red or orange, sometimes brown, and occasionally light orange to light yellow chalcedony is carnelian. Dark red of high intensity is most desirable. The color of grayish stones of low color intensity can sometimes be improved by heating. The brownish shades of this material are generally classified as sard. If the sard is in parallel layers separated by layers of other minerals, the material is called sardonyx and is the birthstone for August. No definite rule exists as to the color line dividing carnelian and sard.

Opaque, dark-green chalcedony spotted with inclusions of red jasper, is bloodstone or heliotrope. The smaller the red jasper spots, the brighter red they are, and the more uniformly they are spaced determines the value of a particular stone. This is the birthstone for March and is much used in signet rings, particularly for men. The term heliotrope stems from an old superstition that the stone, when immersed in water, would turn the image of the sun blood red. To this stone has been ascribed many medicinal uses such as a cure for dyspepsia, a sure remedy for tumors, and an agent for stopping the flow of blood. In addition, the stone has religious significance and is frequently used for carving sacred objects. Traditionally, bloodstone originated at the time of Christ's crucifixion. Drops of blood, drawn by the spear thrust in his side, fell upon a dark green stone at the foot of the cross.

The translucent and leek green—that is, light and grayish yellow-green—variety of cryptocrystalline quartz is prase. If the material is dark green, usually with white or yellowish spots, the variety is plasma. This variety is sometimes used as a substitute for jade.

Banded agate is a term applied to gray, light blue, brown, red, and black chalcedony arranged in curved bands. Many local sub-classifications of banded agate exist. If the bands are arranged in straight parallel layers, the material is properly designated as onyx. Although solid black or green chalcedony without banding is sometimes sold in costume jewelry as onyx, true onyx is always banded.

Clear, usually colorless, chalcedony which will display a rainbow when it is cut in thin sections and polished on both sides is iris agate. Red, green, and blue usually predominate in the rainbow. The phenomenon occurs most often in chalcedony with fine minute lines or bandings in which the thin sections act as a diffraction grating. Relatively few specimens of agate will show this effect.

Chalcedony occurring in the same color as crystalline amethyst is known as amethystine agate. This material is opaque to translucent. Frequently its color is not evenly distributed and is marred by white and yellowish spots. In addition, it has a tendency to fade from exposure to light and heat.

Several forms of chalcedony deposits are of interest. Geodes are hollow shells of chalcedony frequently lined with mineral crystals, usually calcite or quartz. Occasionally the chalcedony shell is partially filled with common opal. Geodes vary in size from a fraction of an inch to three or four feet in diameter. Their shape is usually spherical but depends upon the configuration of the pre-existing cavity in which they formed.

If the chalcedony shell is completely filled with agate, the deposit is called a nodule. Like geodes, they vary widely in size and are usually spherical because the deposit occurred in spherical gas and steam cavities; sometimes nodules are flattened but never angular. An Indian legend purports to explain why nodules are sometimes scattered about over mountain sides. According to this legend, in moments of displeasure and violence the thunder spirits, who lived in volcanic craters hurled the nodules about the surrounding area. Due to this legend nodules are frequently referred to as thunder eggs.

Geodes and nodules contain chalcedony of all varieties. Although there may be a similarity in material from a specific area, very rarely are any two of them identical in color or pattern.

Another chalcedony deposit of distinct interest is its replacement form in the cellular structure of wood and bone. These deposits are designated as petrified wood or petrified bone. Occasionally the deposit occurs in a cavity left by the wood or bone when it decayed. Such a deposit is called a cast. Although in form it resembles the original wood or bone, there is no cellular replacement. As in geode and nodule deposits, all varieties of chalcedony occur in these replacements and casts. The material frequently has additional gem interest, however, because of the cellular patterns or grains of the wood or bone preserved in the agate.

Jasper is an impure, opaque, colored variety of chalcedony. Like agate it has many sub-varieties, most of them too localized to have general usage. A simple variety classification is gen-

Courtesy The Idaho Statesman
Nodule weighing 1,655 pounds recovered by Alfred G. Larson near Pearl

erally used—that is, yellow, red, brown, or green jasper. The use of such a simple classification should not obscure the fact that jasper does occur in numerous patterns, bandings, and color variations. Much petrified wood is jasperized. All varities will take a good, glossy polish, wear well, and in selected specimens are beautifully attractive.

The occurrence of chalcedony is general throughout Idaho. In practically every locality, chalcedony in place or in alluvial deposits can be found. It should be noted, however, that chalcedony generally occurs only in association with acidic formations, usually with rhyolite. Chalcedony is not likely to be found in areas where the country formation is granite or basalt. Areas of particular gem interest are described below.

About twenty miles northwest of Boise on Willow Creek in Ada County, jasper of good quality and a variety of colors occurs in abundance (see Field Trip 6). The best gem quality material comes from a small area on the north side of the west end of Eagle Box Canyon. The jasper here has filled nodules and formed in veins in the rhyolite. It is fine-grained, delicately colored in tints of yellow, purple, pink, and green, and finished specimens display unusual and attractive patterns and scenes.

At the Humming Bird mine in Paris Canyon, Bear Lake County, a red jasper occurs that is dusted full of grains and needles of malachite. The material is close-grained and takes a good polish even though the malachite is considerably softer than the quartz. The contrast of the bright jaspery red and the dark green splotches of malachite is very pleasing in a finished stone. A fine grade of petrified temskya fern comes from the southeastern part of the county along the Wyoming-Utah borders. It is black and the fine, lacy cellular structure of the fern has been preserved.

In Blaine County in the lavas east of the Little Wood River, red and brown jasper occurs in abundance. Only a small percent of this material, unusual in its coloring, is of gem interest. On the Muldoon Summit, particularly on the Carey side, excellent gem quality green moss agate occurs; the moss patterns are fine and lacy.

Red and yellow jasper occurs on Alder Creek in the Mackay district. Geodes and nodules are also found on the ridges of Alder and Antelope Creeks. Many of the geodes, partly filled

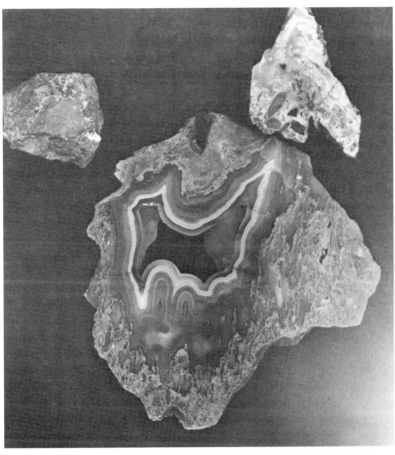

Courtesy Glen and Ruth Evans

Moss agate with fortification, from Carey, Idaho

with agate of interesting bandings, contain pale amethyst or green crystals. The agate in the nodules is of good quality and frequently has patterns or colors of gem interest. Similar geodes and nodules are also found in the lavas near the North Fork of the Lost River. Chalcedony of gem interest occurs the length and breadth of the Pahsimeroi Valley; however, the Mahogany Creek area is probably the most productive. This is an extremely rugged area, and roads are poor. The material is again largely geodes and nodules, but occasional pieces of agate are found. The color of most of the material is a distinctive pink to lavender and frequently displays interesting scenic patterns.

In Fremont County, yellow to brownish-red jasper occurs in the Skull Canyon district. Cubic crystals of galena are included in some of this material.

In Deary, in the Potato Hill area of Latah County, both agate and jasper chalcedony are found. The best gem material is a fine-grained yellow jasper. Although the color is solid and without bandings or patterns, it will take an exceedingly high polish.

The bars of the Salmon River, from Challis to Salmon City in Lemhi County, contain many varieties of chalcedony. The Parker Mountain district and Poison Creek near Salmon are of particular interest. Poison Creek nodules contain green agate and green moss in clear agate.

Chalcedony in abundance occurs in all parts of Owyhee County, particularly in the rhyolite and Payette Lake formations in the county's western portion. Agatized and jasperized petrified wood is found in association with all the ancient Payette Lake Formations. One area of particular interest is Succor Creek: many varieties of chalcedony can be recovered from its gravel bars. The rhyolite cliffs rising on either side of the stream contain geodes, nodules, petrified wood, and chalcedony in veins.

The Graveyard Point locality is particularly noted for its production of fine quality plume agate. The white plumes are long and beautifully formed in a clear agate that takes an excellent polish. Sagenite, tube, and moss agate, and red, blue, and yellow scenic jasper and agate also occur in the area (see Field Trip 7).

Photographed by W. M. Beckert

Petrified wood from the McBride Creek area

Gem quality jasper occurs in an extensive outcropping along Highway 95 in the low foothills approximately ten miles southeast of Marsing, Idaho (see Field Trip 8). The material is an intrusion of chalcedony into the rhyolite of the area. Delicately colored in tints of blue, yellow, brown, pink and green, it is known locally as queenstone. Fashioned gemstones from the material display attractive color patterns resembling landscapes, geometrical figures, and designs. It is fine-grained and solid; consequently, it takes an unusually high polish.

Near the Oregon-Idaho state line to the east of Highway 95 a red to brown and green chalcedony is recovered from State Line Hill (see Field Trip 8). This material, partly agate and partly jasper, is localized in a small area and must now be excavated, as all worthwhile surface material has been picked up. Specimens of this material, having bright and evenly spaced red spots in a green background, fashion into good bloodstones.

Near the canyon of the Bruneau River about twelve miles southeast of Bruneau, Idaho, amethystine agate occurs in pockets over a broad area near the Indian Bathtub on Hot Springs Creek (see Field Trip 9). The agate tends to opal and was possibly deposited by ancient hot springs. The country rock, there, is principally a basic lava intermixed with black and red volcanic cinders. Part of the material is filled with black to brown inclusions or marred by white spots that reduce its gem desirability. However, much of the material is evenly colored and will fashion into attractive stones. As is true with most amethystine material, the color will fade and even turn white from excessive heat or long exposure to sunlight.

Several miles farther up the Bruneau River, a red and green gem-quality jasper, known locally as Bruneau Jasper, is recovered from near the bottom of the canyon walls. Access to the area is easiest from the east side of the canyon (see Field Trip 9). Because the material has undergone the resolidification of double flows, cut specimens display pictures and various geometric patterns.

On Beacon Hill, about twenty miles northwest of Weiser in Washington County, agate nodules, known locally as Beacon Hill thunder eggs, occur in abundance (see Field Trip 5). The

Photographed by W. M. Beckert

Beacon Hill thunder eggs

nodules formed in cavities of the country rhyolite. Some have eroded free of the matrix, but many are still embedded. These nodules are not of uniform quality. Some, only partly agatized and full of holes and soft green and yellow inclusions, have practically no gem interest. Others, when cut, display beautiful bandings in fine and unusual patterns. The color is uniformally gray; however, the material can be permanently dyed many attractive colors. A few contain green and red moss agate of good quality. An occasional nodule contains exquisitely patterned dendrites or sagenites. As the inclusions usually lie in the agate near the outside surfaces of the nodule, it is essential that each be cleaned and the outside shell ground away if necessary to permit thorough examination before cutting; otherwise a valuable gem dendrite or sagenite may be destroyed.

On Hog Creek nearby, similar agate nodules and geodes, weathered free from their matrix, are scattered about over the hillsides of a large area (see Field Trip 5). Most of these have little gem interest, but a few contain agate that has been deposited in wavy patterns of fine bandings. Thin-cut slabs from these nodules, polished on both sides, are beautiful iris agate displaying a strikingly colored rainbow iridescence in transmitted light.

Farther northwest of Weiser, agatized and jasperized petrified wood of excellent gem quality is found in the side canyons and hills on either side of Mann Creek. Much of this material is in small pieces; they are highly colored, however, and ideal for tumbling. The larger pieces, sometimes whole logs, are also highly colored, fine-grained, highly desirable material. In the upper reaches of nearby Sage Creek a good quality petrified wood, mostly red in color, occurs (see Field Trip 5).

Southeast of Weiser on the dumps and in the neighborhood of the mercury mines of the area, bright red cinnabar agate of gem quality occurs. Some specimens are solidly colored; others of greater gem interest are mottled by spots of impurities of various colors. Although the red color of the cinnabar tends to turn black after prolonged exposure to light, stones fashioned from the material are satsifactory over long periods.

The above occurrences of chalcedony in Idaho are far from being all inclusive. The distribution of petrified wood of vary-

Courtesy Alfred G. Larson

Thunder egg diggings at Beacon Hill

ing gem quality, for example, is practically state-wide. There is hardly a locality in the State that does not have a nearby area for the recovery of chalcedony.

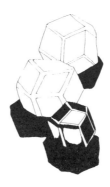

OPAL

OPAL IS A silica mineral containing various amounts of water, usually six to ten percent. Because, with the exception of its water content, the chemical composition of opal is the same as that for quartz, mineralogists frequently classify opal as a variety of quartz. However, because its optical and physical properties are so different from those of quartz, it is usually regarded as a distinct gem species.

Opal occurs in several varieties of gemological importance. These varieties are grouped in three large classifications. Opal varieties of the first group, subdivided into several types, have an iridescent play of color due to the structure of the stone. Black opals, having a black, dark blue, or dark green, or dark gray body color combined with a fine play of color, are the most valuable and are considered by many people to be the most precious of gems. Black opals large enough for brooches and pendants have sold for several thousand dollars each.

White opal, sometimes called Mexican or Australian opal, has a white or light body color with a fine play of color, and is more plentiful and consequently less valuable. However, fine pin-fire white opals are valuable and those with flash fire are desirable.

Opals exhibiting a play of color in rather regular, close-set, angular patches are known as harlequin opals. This term may properly be applied to any opal having this characteristic play of color, although, as a rule, white opals only are designated as harlequin. If the patches of color play are regular and close-set as in the harlequin, but are very small, the opal may be described as pin-fire opal. If the play of color is displayed in more or less irregular bands or streaks, it is described as flame opal or flash-of-fire opal. Some authorities rank opals in value according to their characteristic play of color; however, the type of color play desired is largely a matter of individual taste, and it is difficult to establish whether one type is more preferred than another.

In the second large group of varieties are those opals that display little, if any, play of color. Almost transparent opals of this group, exhibiting a moving, billowy, blue light and having a body color that is milky white or very light tones of various hues, are girasol opals. Those with a milky white body tone are most in demand; but those with body tones of rose, green, and bluish tones are also esteemed.

Transparent to translucent opal, having a body color of orangy-yellow to red or any intermediate hue, or a brownish-orange or brownish-red hue, is fire opal. Transparent bright red is the most valuable type of fire opal. It may or may not have a faint play of color.

Occasionally a fashioned opal cabochon will glow with a pale yellow light over its entire surface. Such opal is known as golden opal. Gem material consisting of alternate layers of gem quality and common opal is onyx opal. Gem material containing some of the mother rock or matrix is designated as opal matrix or opaline.

The third general classification is common opal. It may show a play of color and occasionally is suitable gem material. Prase opal, as the name indicates, is common green opal. Agate opal is material made up of alternate bands of agate and common opal. Milk opal is translucent and milky, with tints of various hues. One type of petrified wood, in which the replacement has been by common opal, is called wood opal. Moss opal is very much like moss agate in appearance. Bluish-white, porcelain-like common opal is cachalong opal. Hydrophane opal is common opal without water. It must be immersed in water or boiled in oil to produce a play of color. Small pieces of hydrophane suspended in glycerine in transparent glass teardrop, or plastic containers are known as floating opal. Hyalite, or Muller's glass, is transparent and colorless common opal; sometimes the term includes translucent and white. Pink opal is usually known as rose opal although, it is sometimes called quinzite. Red to brown common opal is jasper-opal; brown or gray is liver opal or menilite. Waxy or resinous common opal, honey or ocher-yellow, is resin opal. Tabasheer is a variety of common opal that forms in joints of bamboo. Like hydrophane it must be placed in water before its best gem possibilities are displayed. The porous common opal deposited by geysers is geyserite.

Opal doublets are more important than doublets of any other gem species. Sections of gem quality opal otherwise too thin for use can be affixed to a back of common opal with very satisfactory results. The back may also be, and frequently is, chalcedony of various colors, especially black. Sometimes the opal is set into the chalcedony, having a band of the latter around the opal to protect it and enhance its beauty. Occasionally the thin sections of opal are crowned with rock crystal.

Although the ancients believed the opal to be the luckiest of gems for its owner, a superstition of modern times claims that opal is an unlucky gem and likely to bring misfortune to its wearer. This superstitution is now dying. Even though great care must be taken to protect opals because of their lack of toughness and hardness and because they have a tendency to crack as they lose water, they are much in demand by lovers of beautiful gems. Individual opals probably vary more in details of comparative beauty than any other gem. Their countless flashing colors are especially intriguing.

Opal ranging from brown to white, opaque, common opal, through various varieties of semi-opal to fine precious opal, has been found in a number of localities in Idaho.

Opal with play of color cements sandstone from Miocene lake beds on both sides of Mores Creek near Idaho City. Although this area has undergone extensive dredging for gold, remnants of the sandstone formation still exist. Although pieces adequate in size to be cut into gems cannot be recovered, the flashing fire of many small pieces enclosed in a transparent glass or plastic drop as floating opal produces satisfactory results.

In Clark County near Spencer, opal with a beautiful play of color and of excellent quality occurs as seams in rhyolite. The background is transparent to white, while red and green dominate in the play of colors. The locality is under private claim, but digging is permitted on a fee basis. Because the mine is high in the mountains near the Continental Divide, access is possible only during the summer months. The material fashions well in all the cabochon forms common to opal, including doublets and triplets of the thinner pieces.

In August 1890, fine, precious, white opal with a red and green play of color was found while digging a well near Whelan in Latah County, northwest of Moscow almost on the Idaho-Washington state line. The opal occurred more or less frequently from the surface down, and the last four feet of rock, an altered basalt, contained cavities filled with precious opal. Buildings were erected and the locality was named Gem City. From the summer of 1890 through 1904, considerable opal was produced, mostly by the operations of the North American Gem and Opal Mining Company. In quality, the opal recovered was equal to the best of that from Australia. Several of the larger pieces, according to report, were sold for several thousand dollars each. Excellent specimens of this opal are on display at the School of Mines and Geology, University of Idaho.

Today no traces of Gem City exist. The only indication of its approximate location is the Whelan Grange Hall. The country is typical rolling Palouse hills of the area adapted to the growing of wheat. Its present owners are farmers without interest in gem mining and do not welcome the exploration of their property to determine its gem-producing possibilities. Occasionally, however, permission can be secured to work the old dumps. The rock is grayed, weathered, and considerably softened. A few small pieces of precious opal can still be found if enough rock is broken. It is also considered worthy of note that the same vesicular basalt exists as a flow cover-

Courtesy The Idaho Statesman

Prospecting an opal vein

ing large areas of the region. Possibly other nearby discoveries of opal not on private property will be made.

Some very good specimens of dark gray, opalized wood have been found in Latah County near Kendrick in the canyon of the Potlatch River. Vesicles in the lava of the canyon walls below Kendrick are sometimes filled with a milky white common opal, indicative of the possible discovery of opal of gem quality.

In the Pahsimeroi Valley, near May in Lemhi County, common opal of various colors, mostly yellow, flesh pink, and black, occurs in abundance. On the west side of the valley, about six miles from the head of Panther Creek at seven thousand feet elevation, a large dike of porphyry runs parallel to the creek for nearly one and one-half miles, forming a ledge partly covered with overwash but outcropping in many places. This dike is full of opals of all sorts—milky, blue, green, brown, and pink. Some are colorless and transparent, with an excellent play of color in broad flashes. Although the opal frequently occurs in large masses, the porphyry is so very hard that the extraction of large pieces of opal unfractured is very difficult. In addition, the extracted pieces are brittle and very fragile. It is best fashioned by using part of the matrix, which, because of its hardness, takes an attractive polish and protects the opal.

On Clover Creek in Gooding County, near Bliss, opalized wood of fine gem quality has been found. The material is buff to yellow and black, with occasional pieces showing a good play of color. In all of it there is a perfect preservation of the original wood grain. As in the Idaho City area, small veins of opal with a brilliant play of color occur in the Miocene lake sediments which form a part of the country rock of the area. Again these small, brilliantly colored fragments are best displayed as float opal.

Near Lewiston in Nez Perce County, much precious gem opal with a white body color and an excellent predominately red and green play of color has been recovered. The principal source is on the north bank of the Snake River, about ten miles down stream from Lewiston in Whitman County, Washington. A few miles above Lewiston on the Snake River, colorful banded opal is found. The color results from impurities that increase the specific gravity far beyond that usual for opal.

Recovering fire opal at Spencer

Probably for the same reason, it is not brittle and fractured like much common opal. This material will make up into very satisfactory large objects such as book ends and fashion into attractively colored cabochons, some with unusual pictures.

Important discoveries of precious opal were made in Owyhee County very early, about 1893. One of the most important of these early discoveries lies southeast of Givens Hot Springs. Many carats of rough opal, with an excellent play of color and having a transparent blue or white body color, were recovered.

One of the larger mines in this vicinity consisted of two sets of workings on different sides of a small valley, from thirty-five to sixty-five feet above the bottom. Most of the work was done on the west side of the valley, where several cuts fifty feet long and twenty-five feet wide and a tunnel forty feet long were made. Evidence of these old workings is still visible.

A few miles south of Oreana is another of the older opal diggings in Owyhee County that was once highly productive. The material is either transparent or has a white body color with a brilliant display of color. Only occasional finds are made in this area today.

Another Owyhee County occurrence of opal is on a small rounded hill on the west side of Squaw Creek, just below its junction with Little Squaw Creek, about twelve miles from the Oregon State line. The location is near the bottom of the canyon at about 3,500 feet elevation. Characteristic sagebrush-covered hills rise about one thousand feet on either side of the canyon (see Field Trip 8). The basalt at the location is highly vesicular, composed chiefly of lath-shaped crystals of labradorite, augite, and a brownish glass. The basalt is a portion of a flow which partly fills the canyon of Squaw Creek and rests on rhyolite and rhyolite tuff, the principal formation of the region. The basalt is partially disintegrated and breaks up fairly easily. The opal occurs as an amygdaloid in the steam holes and cavities in the basalts and must be patiently picked out. The greater part of the cavities contain no opal and much milky white or colorless common opal. Some of the vesicles are filled with chalcedony and some with banded chalcedony and common opal. Only a small part of the opal is of the precious variety, but some has a fine play of color. The opal at this location has such a high percentage of water that severe

Courtesy Alfred G. Larson
Wangdoodle Fire Opal Mine on Squaw Creek

cracking occurs after drying out, rendering the material value-less. Curing in oil or glycerin is reported to prevent this occurrence.

In the foothills southeast of Homedale and south of Marsing, precious opal with a beautiful sky-blue body color occurs. The two principal diggings for this material are on Poison Creek and at Mule Springs (see Field Trip 8). The Poison Creek location is much the older of the two diggings. Excavations here have been extensive, but a limited amount of excellent material is still being recovered. Because the matrix is a vesicular basalt similar to that at Squaw Creek, material is recovered only through the expenditure of hard work. Digging at the more recently discovered location at Mule Springs is easier, as the opal occurs in a partly decomposed rhyolite. The green, purple and red play of color in opal from both these locations occurs in bands and streaks characteristic of flame or flash of fire opal. Although the attractive blue body color of this material tends to turn white under excessive heating or long exposure to light and drying, it is held in esteem and much sought after.

Common opal and opalized wood in all colors occur throughout Owyhee County. Generally it is of little gem value and is recovered and fashioned into gem stones only incidentally. Dark blue opal, occurring in the rhyolite on the west wall of Succor Creek Canyon and in rhyolite nodules from the Blue Blazes location southeast of Marsing, is hunted and fashioned to some extent. Most of the opalized wood is fashioned into such large ornamental objects as book ends. A favorite and popular digging area lies a few miles southeast of Highway 95 at the Idaho-Oregon State Line. At this locality, known as the Coal Mine Basin, black opalized wood of good quality occurs in a sandstone formation (see Field Trip 8).

Even though much excellent gem opal has been recovered from a number of known localities in the State, few of the diggings have been entirely worked out. The possibility of new discoveries that will also produce equally good material of gemological importance is likely.

GARNETS

Gemologically, the garnets are a related group of gem species. Their chemical composition is usually expressed by the formula $R_2M_2(SiO_4)_3$. R stands for any of the elements magnesium, calcium, manganese or ferrous iron; M for any of the elements aluminum, ferric iron, or chromium. Several of these elements are generally present, and the garnet species, therefore, merge into one another, thus producing a great many types.

Three varieties, pyrope, almandite, and rhodolite, make up the red and purple garnets. Pyrope and almandite are gemologically much more important than rhodolite, which occurs less frequently.

Pyrope usually occurs in an intense blood-red hue, although it also may be found in hues of orangy-red, orange-red, and in lower intensities of brownish-red and red-brown. Garnets occurring in the last two hues are called Bohemian Garnets. Medium to dark red pyropes—those that more nearly approach the color of good rubies—are most valuable. Usually pyropes are much more free of flaws and inclusions than almandites.

Almandite garnet occurs in hues of dark red and purplish-red to reddish-purple and in gem quality is generally known as precious garnet. Sometimes the hues are orange-brown, brownish-orange, red-brown, and brownish-red, similar to those of pyrope. Almandite garnet crystals are most frequently brownish or very dark red. Nearly all are cloudy and have inclusions and flaws. In some localities, as in Alaska, almandite crystals occur in abundance. However, none is of gem quality. The finer quality of almandate, sometimes known as precious garnet, is very beautiful. Some of these gemstones are asteriated. Most exhibit a four-rayed star, while some will display one of six rays, as does corundum. These stones are nearly always translucent and very dark. Their value depends upon the proper orientation and brightness of the star.

Rhodolite occurs in purplish-red to purple hues—that is, a rose-red similar to some almandites. Its chemical composition is between that of pyrope and almandite. Crystals of rhodolite are rare and usually small. Its fine purplish color is exquisite.

The orange, yellow, brown, green and violet garnets occur in three principal varieties. Andradite garnets, transparent yellowish-green to green, are demantoid; transparent yellow, topazolite; and transparent black, melanite. The hue of demantoid is never the true blue-green of emerald; the green always tends to yellowish. However, the nearer the hue approaches that of emerald the more valuable the stone. Demantoid is more brilliant than emerald, and cut stones display fire not possible in emerald. It is also tougher than emerald, but, because its hardness is less than quartz, it will not hold a polish nearly so well as emerald. Topazolite is so rarely found in crystals of gem size that it has no established gem value. Melanite has little gem demand.

Grossularite, a name derived from the Latin word *grossular*, meaning *gooseberry*, occurs in translucent to semi-tranlucent hues of green to yellow and white. Cut gems are known as gooseberry stones. In red-orange, reddish-orange, and red-brown hues, grossularite is called hessonite or hyacinth garnet; in yellow to brown, cinnamon stone. Except as collectors' specimens, grossularite garnets have small gem value. In fact, the green and white hues are often sold for jade, a more valuable gem mineral. Rare hessonite, transparent and vivid

Courtesy Glen and Ruth Evans

Almandite garnet crystals, Idaho's gemstone

orange, is desirable. The majority, however, is badly flawed and not particularly valuable. Cinnamon stone is too common to have much value.

Spessartite garnet occurs in hues of orange-red to orange and also orangy-brown to red-brown, resembling hessonites in color. In its better qualities spessartite facets into a beautiful gemstone.

Uvarovite, the last of the garnet varieties, like topazolite, is rarely found in gem-size crystals. Sometimes its green hue approaches the desirable blue-green hue of emerald. If its occurrence in adequate size were more frequent it would undoubtedly be sought after and valuable.

Garnets as a whole are hard enough and tough enough that they would be more valuable as gemstones if those of inferior quality were not so plentiful, obscuring both the knowledge and appreciation of the beauty of the finer qualities of most varieties. The fact that garnet may occur in almost every color but blue, from deep reds and beautiful violets to emerald greens, is overlooked. Many of these better stones sell for several hundred dollars per carat. For centuries the better quality pyropes and almandites were mistaken for rubies. Many gem lovers consider the bright orange hessonite to be the most beautiful of gemstones. Rare demantoids have been mistaken and even sold for olivines.

Red and purple garnet of the pyrope and almandite varieties occur in situ in many localities and in the placer sands of many parts of Idaho. Only those of known gemological importance are described below.

In Boise County, garnet occurs in abundance in the heavy sands of the placer gold workings in both the Idaho City and Centerville areas. Most are fine grains of sand, but occasional rounded pebbles the size of walnuts are recovered. In some the trapezohedral crystal habit is still recognizable. Even though their hue tends toward brownish-red, they are transparent and a beautiful deep red. In addition, only the more perfect specimens free from flaws and inclusions have survived the stream action. Consequently, most of them are highly satisfactory for the fashioning of gemstones.

In Bingham, Camas, and Clearwater Counties, most of the garnet from placer washings are of sand-grain size only; however, occasional specimens of gem size have been found. The larger pebbles and a few trapezohedral crystals are more usual in the Cow Creek-Pierce district of Clearwater County. These tend to be distinctly purplish-red and are seldom clearly transparent.

Similar purplish-red garnet is abundant in the placer sand concentrates of Elmore County. In Idaho County, garnet is just as plentiful in the sand concentrates, but the hue is brownish-red. In the Warren-Burgdorf area, small pyrope garnets of fair color and good quality are recovered from the placer tailings at both Grouse Creek and Ruby Meadows (see Field Trip 2). At Garnet Rapids on the Salmon River, approximately ten miles above Riggins, small almandite garnets occur in abundance in a mica schist. Although the area has been worked extensively, the crystals are opaque, friable, and of little gem value.

Latah County is world-famous as the source of almandite crystals that will produce asteriated gemstones. Many excellent gem crystals have been recovered from several sources on the East Fork of Emerald Creek. The area is about five miles from the junction of the Emerald Creek road with the main highway from Fernwood to Clarkia (see Field Trip 1). The garnets occur in matrix in mica schist as rhombic dodecahedron, trapezohedron, or a combination of these crystal habits. The crystals range from very small to as much as three inches in diameter.

The mica schist matrix at these locations breaks up with fair ease. Care should be taken, however, to protect the crystals from injury during their extraction. These crystals have a high degree of internal strain and chip and crack when subjected to heat, pressure, or blows, even those stresses arising from the fashioning and mounting processes. Many of the crystals also have inclusions that further reduce their toughness.

Stones cut from Emerald Creek crystals are dark purple, light purple, or dark red. Their value in relation to their size depends entirely upon the brightness of the star, its number of rays, and its proper orientation with the rays intersecting exactly at the apex of the cabochon. Since a star lies directly beneath the center of each diamond-shaped face of the crystal, each crystal, if polished as a sphere, will display twelve four-rayed stars. Generally there is a noticeable degree of brightness in the stars. Therefore, the face displaying the brightest star should be chosen for the cutting of an individual stone, provided that it does not contain inclusions or fractures that would make the selection of a face with a weaker star advisable. The proper orientation of the star is fairly easy in an individual stone cut from a complete crystal. The base of the cabochon must be cut exactly parallel to the crystal face selected, and the apex of the cab must be in the center of the face. The asterism in garnets, as in other star stones, is caused by inclusions called silk. The examination of the cut cross-section of most garnet crystals reveals that the silk is not evenly distributed throughout the crystal but lies in layers. Since the maximum brightness of the star is displayed when the face of a cabochon is in a silk layer, weak stars may be strengthened by deeper grinding. Conversely, a bright star may be weakened by too deep grinding that goes through the layer of silk into a layer of non-silk. Experience alone is the guide in determining when a silk layer has been reached and maximum brightness of the star attained.

Care must be taken throughout the fashioning process to prevent the stone's being heated or subjected to sudden changes of temperature; otherwise, it will blister or possibly develop a deeper fracture.

If the cabochon is cut with a high crown, the star will stay on top of the stone when it is tilted back and forth. The more shallow the cabochon, the more liquid the star becomes and the more rapidly it will move across the face of the stone.

The stream bed of Emerald Creek is red with garnet, and large areas have been dredged to recover the garnet for commercial abrasives. Broken crystals of gem quality and size can be recovered from the creek bed and dredge tailings. A second Latah County source of good gem-quality star garnet material is a location on Purdue Creek, north of Bovill (see Field Trip 1). The garnet here is recovered as water-worn crystal fragments or rolled pebbles from the gem gravels of the creek bed. Because of the high specific gravity of the garnet, it has a tendency to work down and is found in greater abundance as bed rock is approached.

Photographed by W. M. Beckert
Almandite garnet crystals and starred cabochons from Emerald Creek

The gem quality of the Purdue Creek material is high, as only the more perfect pieces free from weakening inclusions, fractures, and feathers have survived the stream action. However, the proper orientation of the star in the finished stone is much more difficult to obtain.

Garnets, purplish rose-red almost to pink, also occur in pegmatites in the mica and beryllium mines near Avon in Latah County. Few of these are of gem quality; most are much traversed by checks and are friable, granular, and opaque.

In Lemhi County, almandite garnet occurs in several places in schists. Although the crystals are well formed and sometimes are almost an inch in diameter, few are of gem quality and none are asteriated.

Brownish-red and purplish-red garnet crystals are abundant in the placer concentrates and sand of the Snake River in Minidoka County. Only rarely is a crystal of gem size recovered, however.

In Nez Perce County, rose-red and brown-red garnet crystals occur in placer concentrates of the Clearwater River. A number of fine purple almandite stones of excellent gem quality have been recovered from the river sands between Orofino and Lewiston.

In the Silver City area of Owyhee County, purplish-red trapezohedral garnet crystals occur in a scattered aggregate of mica and feldspar (see Field Trip 10). Although most of these crystals are small, they are sharp and perfect. Some of the larger crystals, almost an inch in diameter, are of gem quality.

Crystals of reddest garnet are abundant in the contact metamorphic zones surrounding the intrusive mass of monazite north of Canyon Creek, in the Coeur d'Alene district of Shoshone County. Garnet is extensively developed in the metamorphosed Belt sediments where they approach the central Idaho batholith on the St. Joe-Clearwater divide of Shoshone County.

The brown to green garnets, sometimes referred to by mineralogists as the Andradite-Grossularite Series, or simply as the lime garnets, occur in several places in Idaho with contact metamorphic minerals in limestone silicate zones adjacent to igneous intrusions.

Courtesy Dixie Douglas

Working gem gravels for garnets on Emerald Creek

These lime garnets have been considered of interest and some economic importance because of their frequent association with valuable bodies of ore. The gem quality of these Idaho garnets has never been evaluated nor determined.

In the Seven Devils area of Adams County, lime garnets occur in silicate contact zones in limestone mined for copper. Some crystal specimens are comparable to the best found in the world. Andradite crystals occur embedded in glassy copper-stained quartz from which they easily separate, leaving beautiful, sharp crystals up to one inch in diameter.

On Lanes Creek in Bear Lake County, lime garnets are associated with hematite and calcite in metamorphosed limestone.

In the Muldoon district of Blaine County, lime garnets occur near Ketchum. These crystals are of poor quality, being friable and filled with inclusions, mostly calcite.

Lime garnets occur in Custer County in Phi Kappa Canyon near the head of Big Lost River. On a round knob 8,700 feet high, just west of where the road from Ketchum to Mackay crosses Trail Creek summit, and across Park Creek, is a formation containing abundant lime garnet. In the Copper Basin district at the head of Big Lost River, lime garnets are abundant in lime silicates. In the Alder Creek district, lime garnet is the most abundant mineral in contact copper deposits near Mackay. Most of it is massive.

On the Frank Mortimer property on Iron Mountain northeast of Weiser, an extensive outcropping of grossularite garnet occurs. The crystals vary in size, the larger ones measuring an inch in diameter. The yellowish-green color is that characteristic of grossularite. However, the crystals are not transparent and are friable from exposure. It is possible that crystals of good gem quality could be recovered by development and exploration of this outcrop.

Because of its abundance and wide distribution throughout the State, garnet is one of the principle gem minerals sought after by gem hunters. This, and the high gem quality of the Emerald Creek almandite garnet, has resulted in the garnet's being chosen as the Idaho state gemstone. Interest in the material should grow as the very probable discovery of new localities is made and old ones are further developed. A little time spent working gravel bars of most streams in the State yields satisfying results.

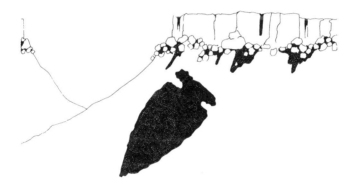

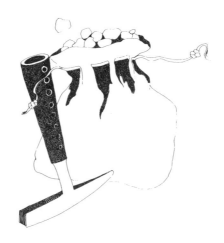

CORUNDUM

Ruby and Sapphire

THE ALUMINIUM OXIDE mineral corundum is widespread throughout the world. Next to diamond it is the hardest known naturally occurring mineral. Prior to the manufacture of carborundum, common corundum, known as emery, was extensively used as an abrasive.

Gem quality corundum is comparatively rare and is limited to a few world-wide localities. It occurs in all shades and tones of practically every color. Transparent material of medium to dark tones of red to purplish-red hues, popularly described as pigeon-blood red, is ruby. In its finest qualities, ruby is the most valuable of gemstones. Its history as a gem is long and interesting, and it has always been held in esteem and treasured above all other gems. It is known as the gem of the sun and is usually accepted as the birthstone of July. It is emblematic of affection, power, and majesty. To it is attributed the power of making its owner fearless and able to achieve victory. Loss of color in a ruby is supposedly a warning of impending danger to its owner, the true color returning when the danger is over.

Corundum gemstones of all colors other than pigeon-blood red are sapphires. The most desired color is cornflower blue. Perfection in this color lies in a hue between violet-blue and violetish-blue. Sapphire is symbolic of truth and constancy. A special virtue attributed to the star sapphire is that it wards off all evil forces and protects its wearer from all malignant influences.

Corundum has been discovered in several localities in Idaho. All are in alluvial deposits; none in situ, probably because all discoveries have been incidental to gold placer and dredging operations. Only a very small percentage of the corundum discovered is of gem quality.

In Clearwater County near Pierce, in the locality where gold was first discovered in Idaho, corundum is found in the gold-bearing gravels, particularly along Rhodes and Orofino Creeks. Opaque dull-gray material predominates as usual, none of which approaches gem quality. However, diligent search is usually rewarded by the finding of a few transparent light-blue and light bluish-green stones. Occasionally stones of deeper shades of blue are found. Some crystals have a blue sapphire core in a grayish to greenish shell of common corundum. All this transparent material is satisfactory for facet cutting of fine gems. In addition, much of the translucent to semi-translucent material—mostly pinkish-gray—if cut in cabochon will display a chatoyancy and an occasional asterism, and make up into attractive and desirable stones.

The crystals are rough, imperfect, worn, and occasionally coated with muscovite, a pearly white mica. Most of them are simple hexagonal prisms terminated by a basal pinacoid, but some are the double hexagonal pyramids, a crystal habit of gem sapphire.

In Custer County, corundum has been discovered in many of the gold placers of the Stanley Basin. In Valley County, it occurs in the gold placers of Gold Fork and other tributaries of the Payette River. The tailings of old gold placer workings at Paddy Flat on Gold Fork creek, northeast of Donnelly, are a popular and productive hunting locality.

Near the old town of Resort in Idaho County, on Secesh

Courtesy Alfred G. Larson
Working gem gravels for sapphires at Rocky Flat

Sapphire mine at Rocky Flat

Creek between Warren and Burgdorf, common corundum is abundant in the gold placers. Near the mouth of Grouse Creek, long windrows of hand-picked boulders of old placers extend from the mountains over the flat valley floor, among stunted jack pine. The corundum here was so abundant that it boiled the sluice boxes of the gold miners, interfering with gold recovery. A search among the boulders of any of the windrows will yield results. The crystals are more plentiful, however, at places where cleanups were made.

Across the Secesh at Ruby Meadows is another excellent hunting locality. Great scars exist on the mountains where thousands of tons of material were washed away in the search for gold. As at Grouse Creek, the corundum crystals are recovered by reworking the piles of debris heaped high on the valley floor.

Crystals recovered from these localities are mostly broken; however, they are not so worn that their hexagonal crystal structure has been entirely obliterated. This is fortunate because most of the material must be dry-screened, and the crystals handpicked by recognition of their crystal form and sheen. Most of the crystals are common gray corundum of little or no gem value, but a few translucent to transparent blue crystals of gem quality are obtainable and many of the opaque pinkish-gray and bronze crystals will cut into desirable stones with an attractive chatoyant luster.

In Adams and Valley Counties between McCall and Meadows, on the headwaters of Goose Creek, is perhaps the most widely known and most explored corundum locality in Idaho. The area, known as the Rocky Flat placers, has been exploited for various minerals (see Field Trip 2). Extensive development work has been done. A tunnel was once drilled through the mountain that extends as a spur between the upper reaches of Goose Creek and the canyon leading to Meadows. Sluice boxes were placed in the tunnel and much material was washed. This tunnel is now partly caved in and abandoned. A large glory hole, filled with water, marks its head at the placer area. According to report, the company that did this extensive work was mining for diamonds. Rumor says that a few octahedron diamond crystals were recovered. If any were recovered, the number was not sufficient to warrant continued working.

Courtesy Alfred G. Larson
Handpicking sapphires from gem gravels at Rocky Flat

The corundum here is abundant in association with numerous garnets, quartz crystals, and occasional crystals of many other such minerals as topaz, tourmaline, spinel, and hematite, as well as crystals of several non-gem varieties. Although some of the corundum crystals display the hexagonal prismatic habit of corundum, most are broken and water worn, indicating the long presence of these very tough and hard crystals in the gem gravels. Gray and amethyst shades predominate, but small pink and cornflower blue stones yielding cut gems of from one-half to one carat, as well as inky blue stones, can be found. A few ruby crystals of poor color have been recovered—all are either too light red or too red-brown to be accurately classified as rubies. Most of the corundum is the common non-gem variety, opaque and dull gray and brownish in color. Much of this material, however, has a silky sheen or opalescence and will make star or chatoyant cabs. Excellent sapphires of highly desirable gem quality come from material recovered at this location.

Mining methods are primitive. Because of its high specific gravity corundum concentrates in pockets near bedrock with other heavy minerals. It can be further concentrated by running the crystal-bearing material through a sluice box, but eventually each crystal must be hand picked from the gem gravels. A fine-meshed screen is generally used. This permits the washing or sifting away of dirt, sand and all gravel containing crystals too small to be of value. Most corundum has a bright sheen when wet. Consequently, if the material is hand picked in bright sunshine, this sheen makes for ease of identification, even though the crystal form may be completely worn away.

Because the mineral is so hard, the equipment used by amateur lapidaries is generally inadequate for the finishing of corundum gems. A stone can be rough-shaped with a carborundum wheel, but the final sanding and polishing is best accomplished with lap plates or wheels charged with diamond dust.

Although much synthetic gem corundum is now manufactured, natural stones have maintained their desirability. The finding of a stone that will cut into a gem of good quality and fine color is a particularly satisfying experience. Such a find is possible in Idaho.

BERYL

BERYL, A SILICATE of aluminum and beryllium, is one of the most important of the gem minerals because the variety occurring in vivid medium and dark tones of green, slightly tinged with blue, is emerald. The finest quality emeralds have a soft body appearance and are not clearly transparent. A flawless emerald is very rare; many are mossy because of faulty crystallization and most have inclusions of other minerals as mica and tourmaline. Because gem quality emerald does not occur in large crystals, stones larger than three carats are comparatively more valuable. Fine emeralds in large size are almost as expensive as fine rubies and are more valuable than comparable diamonds.

Usually accepted as the birthstone for May, the emerald, according to tradition, represents immortality, exalted faith, and endows its owner with the power to gain victory over trial and sin. To the early Christians, the emerald was symbolic of the Resurrection. Prior to the Christian era, the gem was sacred to Venus, Goddess of Love, and was emblematic of kindness and good-heartedness.

Because the emerald is so fragile and requires the utmost skill to develop each stone's possibilities to the full, emerald cutters consider themselves the aristocracy of their trade. These cutters believe that the flaws inherent in nearly every fashioned gem enhance its individual beauty. They refer to the flaws as *Jardin,* the French word for *garden.* The legend is that ancient fortune tellers, by gazing deeply into and study ing intently the foliage of the *Jardin,* could foretell the fortune of the gem's owner.

Other varieties of beryl occur in light tones of many colors and a few in the darker tones of blue and red. Next to the emerald, the light blue to light bluish-green variety of aquamarine is most desired. Darker blue stones are known as Madagascar aquamarines. Light golden-yellow is golden beryl; yellow and brown, helidor; greenish-yellow, chrysolite beryl; light red to light purple (pink, lilac, rose, raspberry) is morganite. The colorless variety of beryl, goshenite, has little gem value.

Unlike emerald, the other varieties of beryl may occur in exceedingly large crystals that are generally quite flawless. Therefore, the price per carat of stones cut from these other varieties does not increase with their size. Stones cut from these varieties, consequently, are particularly suitable for brooches and rings where large stones are desired.

Aquamarine, the birthstone for March, is well known and readily available as there is a large world supply coming principally from Brazil. Aquamarine, as well as the other varieties of beryl, has a characteristic beauty. This, together with the hardness of the mineral species making possible the taking and retaining of a high polish, causes stones of all varieties to be highly desirable.

There have been a few important discoveries of beryl in Idaho. Because it is so brittle, it cannot last in gem gravels. Unlike corundum, it must be found in place. In Latah County near Avon, between Deary and Princeton, beryl occurs with feldspar and quartz in pegmatites of the mica schist. The crystal habit is prismatic, common to minerals that crystalize in the hexagonal system. These prismatic crystals are sometimes two to three inches in diameter and seven to eight inches long. The prismatic planes are fairly smooth but the terminations are incomplete. The chrysolite beryl variety is pale greenish-yellow. Many of the crystals are opaque but some of gem quality are translucent to transparent. Usually the crystals are so greatly fractured and iron-stained that only small stones can be fashioned. The mines have been worked for beryllium, and mica, not gems; the methods of mining may account for the shattering of many of the crystals. In mining for beryl gems of any variety, explosives are little used and extreme care is taken to protect the crystals from breakage.

Recently an important discovery of dark blue, gem-quality beryl was made by George H. D. Ogden, one of the few old time prospectors still living and active who, on foot and alone, comb the wilderness areas of Idaho for its mineral wealth. The discovery, lying in the primitive area near Atlanta in Elmore county, has not yet been fully developed nor defined. The occurrence is in a pegmatite in granite similar to the mineralized pegmatite at Dismal Swamps. The beryl is associated in the pegmatite with crystals of feldspar, smoky quartz, some topaz, and rare earth minerals. A substantial number of crystals two to six inches long and one-half to three-quarters of an inch in diameter have been recovered. Although these are very adequate in size for gem cutting, no exceedingly large crystals have yet been found. The crystals are well formed, the faces smooth, but the terminations are incomplete. They are transparent and free from inclusions and flaws. The distinctive dark blue color and quality are superb for gem cutting. A few small crystals of the same color have been recovered from a beryllium deposit on Sheep Creek, a tributary of the Middle Fork of the Boise River.

Rumors persist of the occurrence of light blue aquamarine and pink morganite in various localities in Idaho. Conditions favorable to the formation of beryl exist in the mica schists of northern Idaho and in the pegmatites in the granites of central Idaho. Future discoveries of gem-quality beryl are highly probable, particularly since the quest for beryllium, in response to newly developed uses and commercial demand, has been much intensified.

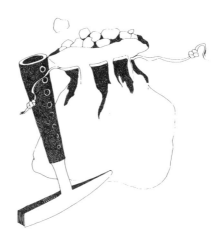

TOPAZ

TOPAZ, A BASIC aluminum silicate mineral, occurs in a wide range of colors. Colorless crystals are found naturally and can be produced by heating crystals of certain colors. Stones cut brilliant from colorless topaz are called slave's diamonds. Pale greenish-yellow to yellowish-green crystals are chrysolite topaz. Slightly orangy-yellow to golden- yellow topaz, the most popular variety, is Brazilian topaz. Brownish-yellow crystals are sherry topaz; dark orange to dark orange-red, hyacinth topaz; light to very light blue, blue topaz. Light violet, resembling pale amethyst, is the rare variety, violet topaz.

Light red to light purplish-red crystals are known as rose or pink topaz. This variety, rarely found naturally, is produced by heating sherry or brownish-yellow crystals. The heating process is called pinking, and the resulting material is commonly referred to as pinked topaz. The color of pinked topaz is permanent.

Red topaz is an extremely rare variety, but authenticated finds are on record. All colors of topaz, except yellows, brown, and reds, are light to very light or pale in tone.

The pastel color tones of topaz are particularly attractive to women. This, plus the fact that the gem lacks toughness because it cleaves easily in a plane parallel to the base of the crystal, accounts for the gem's being regarded as feminine.

The yellow variety of topaz is the most popular and is usually accepted as the November birthstone. However, because topaz lacks toughness, citrine quartz largely replaces it, particularly as a ring stone.

Much topaz contains feathers, flaws, and liquid or gaseous inclusions. However, a fine clean stone of good color is an exceptionally beautiful gem. The hardness of eight on Moh's scale makes it possible for the stone to take and retain a high polish. In addition, most fashioned topaz exhibits a soft, diffused, or velvety body appearance that enhances its beauty and increases its desirability.

Topaz may occur almost anywhere other gem minerals are found. It is associated with the gem minerals tourmaline, quartz, fluorite, apatite, beryl, and with tungsten and tin ores. Like beryl, usually it is discovered in situ in gneisses, schists, and pegmatites. It is occasionally recovered from gem gravels, particularly in the vicinity of the matrix and where stream action has not been too severe.

In Idaho, topaz occurs on Camas Creek in Clark County in colorless and pale yellow crystals up to one-quarter inch in diameter and from one-quarter to one-half inch in length.

Finds of blue topaz have been reported from the gold-bearing gravel at Paddy Flat, on Gold Fork Creek in Valley County, near Donnelly.

A limited amount of colorless topaz is associated with aquamarine beryl in the pegmatite above Atlanta in Elmore County.

The most notable topaz-producing locality is at Dismal Swamp, also in Elmore County. The area lies northwest of Rocky Bar. About nine-and-one-half miles on the road from Rocky Bar to Trinity Lakes, the Buck Creek forest trail branches off toward the Middle Fork of the Boise River. This trail leads directly to the Swamp. A rough road leading to the area takes off the main road about one-quarter mile above the Buck Creek Trail (see Field Trip 4).

Topaz crystals, usually colorless but occasionally pink and of fine clear quality, one-fourth to two inches long, occur in pegmatites in the granite and in alluvial gravels near the swamp. The topaz is associated in the pegmatite with smoky quartz, feldspar, and rare earth and radioactive minerals.

Because of its frequency of occurrence, other discoveries of gem-quality topaz are probable.

Courtesy J. V. Root
Digging for quartz and topaz crystals at Dismal Swamp

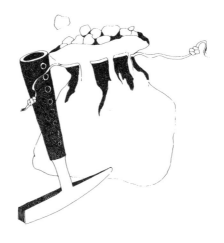

MISCELLANEOUS GEM MINERALS

APATITE

The phosphate mineral apatite, colorless when pure, occurs in violet, light blue, yellow, light red, brown, and various hues of green crystals. Its crystal habit is a hexagonal prism; a few crystals are long but most are short and stumpy.

The occurrence of gem quality apatite is notable from a few Idaho locations. In the Blackbird mining district of Lemhi County, small yellow crystals occur. Long, slender, white prisms of apatite are also found embedded in the quartz associated with the cobalt of the same location.

Because apatite is the most widely distributed of the mineral phosphates and occurs in many rocks, principally in pegmatites in igneous or metamorphic rocks, further discoveries in Idaho are probable.

CALCITE

Although calcite ranks only three in hardness, it does have gem interest because it occurs in an almost endless variety of forms and colors. Transparent crystals or masses facet into

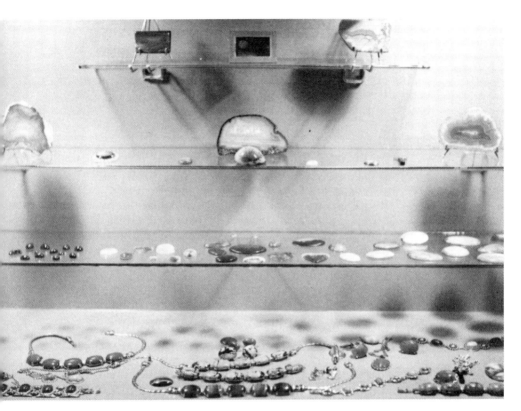

Gemstones from the author's collection

stones with a vitreous luster; however, its most popular use is for the carving of ornamental art objects.

Calcite is one of the most abundant of all minerals and is found almost everywhere in Idaho. In the drier desert areas, it occurs as well defined crystals and incrustations in cavities in the rocks. In the limestone caves of southeastern Idaho the stalactites and stalagmites are calcite. Sometimes these are colored by impurities and banded, resulting in calcite onyx. Also, in smaller cavities in these caves beautiful crystals grow. At the sites of dry and existing hot springs, massive deposits of calcite known as travertine frequently occur with attractive bandings and colors.

CASSITERITE

The tin dioxide, cassiterite, occurs in veins in granite and as rolled pebbles in alluvial deposits. Generally it is black or brown and opaque. That best suited for gem purposes is translucent to transparent and brown, reddish-brown, yellow or green-yellow. It is hard enough to take and retain a high polish, and finished stones have an attractive high adamantine to metallic luster.

Occasional pieces of cassiterite suitable for gem cutting occur in two localities in Idaho. In Lemhi County, stream tin occurs in Silver Creek and along Panther Creek near its junction with Moyer Creek. The mineral in both these deposits occurs in sizes from small, round grains to pebbles one-half inch or more in diameter. Most of the rolled pebbles have a radiate fibrous structure and vary from pale brown and red-brown to black. In the placers of the Silver City District of Owyhee County, rounded pebbles of cassiterite one-eighth to one-half inch in diameter occur, especially along Jordan Creek (see Field Trip 10). The predominate color here is yellowish-brown or tan.

COPPER MINERALS

Three brightly colored idiochromatic minerals of the copper family having gem interest occur in Idaho. Azurite, a copper carbonate, is characterized by its intense, deep blue color. Almost invariably it is associated with malachite, a beautiful emerald to grass-green copper carbonate. Malachite is more abundant than azurite, since it is a more stable compound, and azurite tends to change to malachite. A cabochon displaying the color combination of both minerals has unusual gem interest.

Both minerals usually occur in massive form. Frequently the massive pieces of malachite have bandings, increasing their gem interest. In other pieces, needle-like, included crystals of the mineral radiate in a fibrous mass from a center, giving a silky luster to a finished stone.

The third copper mineral is chrysocolla, a hydrous copper silicate. It is an intense blue-green, rivaling turquoise in color.

None of these three minerals, least of all chrysocolla, are hard enough to take and retain a good polish, nor do they possess the durability generally required of a gem mineral. They are fashioned, instead because of their beautiful colors. Furthermore, malachite and chrysocolla have great staining power, and quartz is easily colored a vivid green by a very small percentage of either.

All three minerals are found in many localities in Idaho. None is dependable for furnishing fine specimens in large number, but occasional good material comes from all of them. Each is an important ore mineral in the oxidized zones of most copper mines. In Adams County, all three minerals occur as stains and incrustations in the many copper mines of the Seven Devils district. Fine specimens have also been recovered from the copper mines of the Fort Hall district of Bannock County, the Wood River district of Blaine County, the Alder Creek district of Custer County, the Hoodoo district of Latah County, the Blackbird district of Lemhi County, the copper mining districts of Shoshone County, and from the mine dumps of South Mountain in Owyhee County.

EPIDOTE

Epidote is a hydrous silicate of calcium and aluminum with varying proportions of ferric iron. It occurs in prismatic crystals, fibrous aggregates, and granular masses. Most epidote is light yellowish-green, known as pistachio green; however, some are other tones of yellow-green, black, or brown. It may be transparent, translucent, or opaque. The transparent crystals are faceted brilliant, step, or mixed cuts.

Epidote is widespread in its occurrence in Idaho. The dumps of the copper mines in the Seven Devils district of Adams County are again productive. Some of the epidote crystals here are embedded in quartz of a later growth. Crystals and large massive pieces are scattered in abundance over the hill south of the old Kleinschmidt grade on the first ridge east of the Snake River. Epidote has also been recovered incidental to the recovery of corundum in the Pierce area of Clearwater County. Occasional finds are made from the mine dumps of the Silver City district of Owyhee County. In Valley County, in the foothills northeast of Donnelly and north of the Paddy Flat road, it occurs with clear quartz crystals. Also in Valley County north of McCall, west of the road to Burgdorf, it occurs in abundance in a deposit of marble, limestone, and garnet. Occasional crystals are found in High Valley, north and east of Ola (see Field Trip 3).

Much epidote is friable, and crystals cleave easily. Flawless material suitable for gem cutting is rare; some of it, however, will cut into very desirable stones. Some cut stones have a special gem interest because they are highly trichroic in the colors of green, yellow, and brown.

FELDSPAR

Like the garnets, the feldspars are a group of closely related mineral species. As a group, they are the most common minerals in the earth's crust; they are ever-present as a constituent of all igneous rocks, and common clay is largely decomposed feldspar.

Several gem varieties of the feldspar minerals are important. Moonstone, sometimes designated as precious moonstone or adularia, is an orthoclase feldspar. It is clear, with a floating billowy light known as adularescence. The more bluish the sheen the greater the value becomes. The finest of the moonstones are far superior in beauty to those yielded by other feldspars and minerals.

Sunstone, also known as aventurine feldspar, is greenish, brownish, or whitish with a golden-reddish, spangled effect known as aventurescence. This phenomenon is caused by inclusions of a glistening variety of hematite or goethite. Trans-

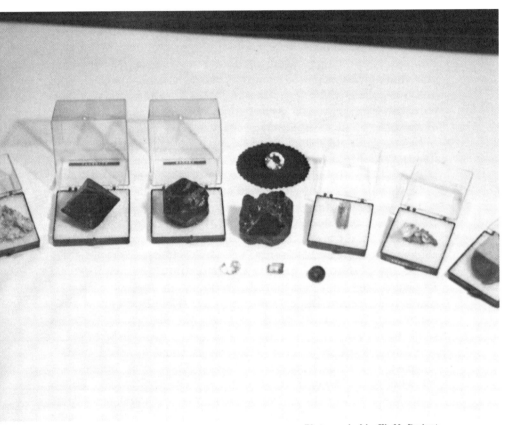

Photographed by W. M. Beckert

Idaho gem crystals and faceted stones

parent sunstone with a deep yellow-orange color is the most desirable and valuable.

Another gem variety of the feldspar minerals is labradorite, displaying a greenish, bluish, yellowish, or reddish change of colors as the stone is moved. Amazonite, a light bluish-green, is still another variety. Noticeable laminations, white streaks, and cracks occur frequently. In its better qualities, however, it will cut and polish into an attractive and desirable gem. Finally, orthoclase feldspar produces a transparent to light yellow material resembling light-colored citrine quartz. This material, either cabbed or faceted, takes a good polish and has an attractive, soft body appearance, somewhat like the effect of alcohol mixed with water.

In Camas County near Fairfield, moonstone of excellent quality occurs. Finished stones are clear and display a beautiful blue adularescence. Finished stones of this material on display in the Idaho Statehouse are of the finest quality.

The clear to pale yellow feldspar occurs in many places in Idaho. In Boise County, it is a constituent of coarse pegmatites and veins in the granite, particularly near Shafer Creek and Idaho City. In Lemhi County, rounded orthoclase crystals occur in the granite and granite gneiss of the Blackbird district. In places they have weathered free from the mother rock and strew the ground like pebbles. Similar crystals occur in pegmatites in the granite of the Silver City district of Owyhee County.

A locality of particular interest is Crystal Butte, about eighteen miles north of St. Anthony. Here, clear plagioclase feldspar crystals occur in abundance. The rock of the Butte is andesite or basalt, having a dense, black ground mass containing scattered large and well formed phenocrysts of transparent plagioclase. Many of these phenocrysts have broken free and clutter the surface, giving rise to the name Crystal Butte. They vary from colorless to pale yellow, and those not stained by infiltrated iron oxide or filled with fractures are of good gem quality.

Although feldspar gems are exceptional neither in toughness nor hardness, the finer specimens are exceedingly beautiful. Few of Idaho's amateur gemologists are fully aware of the gem possibilities of readily available feldspars. As interest grows, it may be discovered that Idaho has much more material of gem interest than is now of record.

FLUORITE

The calcium fluoride mineral, fluorite, crystallizes in the cubic system and is therefore isotropic. It is translucent to transparent and has an easy, perfect octahedron cleavage. Fashioning is difficult because of this easy cleavage, and it must be handled with extreme care. Because it is so soft, polished stones soon lose their polish and luster. It does, however, have interesting properties that recommend it as a gem mineral. Much fluorite will fluoresce, and occasionally a specimen will phosphoresce. Further, it occurs in many attractive colors— yellow, green, orange, blue, red, violet, pink, and brown. Sometimes specimens are mottled or multi-colored. In addition to gem stones, it is fashioned into such ornamental objects as vases, paperweights, and figurines. Sometimes the perfect octahedron cleavages are used in jewelry without fashioning.

Two localities in Idaho are noted for the occurrence of fluorite. It occurs in veins and pegmatites in the ore body of the copper mines in the Alder Creek district of Custer County. Large, colorless to light purple pieces weighing several pounds can be recovered from the mine dumps. Fluorite also occurs as veins and pegmatites in the ore body at Stibnite in Valley County and can be recovered from the mine dump in large pieces of light purple, violet, and light green.

HEDENBERGITE AND ILVAITE

Two comparatively rare minerals, Hedenbergite and Ilvaite, occur as associate minerals with the many minerals of South Mountain in Owyhee County (see Field Trip 11). Both have only minimum gem interest and are generally cut by collectors. Hedenbergite is a brownish-green opaque mineral that occurs in masses of radiating needle-like crystals. Consequently a cabochon cut from it usually has a pleasing chatoyancy, but it is neither tough nor hard enough to be used as a gem. Ilvaite is black and occurs as stubby opaque prismatic crystals. Stones faceted from ilvaite have a high metallic luster and are durable; but because they are opaque, they lack the brilliancy desired in a faceted stone.

HEMATITE

The iron oxide hematite occurs in steel gray, brown, and black varieties. In the gem trade, black hematite is sometimes referred to as "black diamond," particularly that from Alaska. The mineral is called hematite because it leaves a red streak and is blood-red when powdered or viewed in thin sections in transmitted light. Liquid coolants used in fashioning processes for the mineral are also quickly colored red.

Hematite is faceted and cut cabochon. Occasional specimens having a fibrous structure will display a chatoyancy if cut cabochon. One of the most popular cuts is intaglio ring stones for men.

Much hematite occurs throughout Idaho, but only a limited amount of it is of gem quality. Crystalline lenses always have a gem possibility. Although hematite usually occurs in sedimentary iron ore deposits, it is likely to be present in many types of deposits. In Adams County it is abundant in association with the copper ores of the Seven Devils district. The dumps of the old mines are a probable source of material. Hematite is recovered as rolled pebbles from the gravel bars of Lane's Creek in Bannock County. Its occurrence has been reported from an area about two miles southeast of Bloomington in Bear Lake County. Large, rolled pebbles of hematite occur in the placers of the Boise Basin in Boise County. The dumps of old copper mines in the Alder Creek district of Custer County have been productive. A great body of hematite occurs in Washington County on Iron Mountain about six miles east of the old town of Mineral. Only an occasional piece, however, is of gem interest. A deposit of good gem quality occurs on Iron Mountain in Latah County about twenty miles north of Moscow. The hematite here occurs in botryoidal masses of the desirable black that finishes with brilliance and a high metallic luster. Nearly all of it has a fibrous banded structure that gives chatoyancy to a finished cabochon.

Gem hunters should always be on the lookout for hematite whenever alluvial deposits are being worked in Idaho. Isolated finds, incidental to the search for other minerals, have been made at Rocky Flat on Goose Creek, from the Grouse Creek placers of Idaho County, and other places of gem interest.

JADE

Many discoveries of jade in Idaho have been reported, but the only authenticated source is on Bitch Creek in Fremont County, a few miles north of Tetonia. The jade occurs as rolled boulders in the creek bed. The best method of recovery is to wade in the stream searching for the black or dark green boulders with the slick, greasy appearance of rough jade when wet. The jade here ranges in quality from poor to medium, with an occasional piece of excellent gem quality.

KYANITE

Kyanite, an aluminum silicate mineral, occasionally occurs in Idaho in gem quality as long, flattened crystals. These blade-like crystals form in metamorphic rocks commonly in association with garnet and staurolite. Transparent crystals of good color—blue, grey, green, or brown—can be faceted to advantage.

Kyanite is of special interest as a mineral because of the extraordinary variation of hardness according to direction. The crystal blades, grained almost like wood, are only four to five in hardness in the direction of length and can be scratched with a steel knife blade. Across the grain, however, the hardness is six to seven.

The only important locality for the occurrence of kyanite of gem quality in Idaho is in Shoshone County. It has frequently developed in metamorphosed rocks of Belt series in the southern portion of the County, especially south and east of Avery. It occurs in mica schists on the divide between the headwaters of the St. Joe and Clearwater Rivers. Pale blue and green crystals, some six to seven inches long, occur in a locality two to three miles south of the Trimmed Tree Mountain.

OBSIDIAN

The natural glass obsidian is found generally throughout Idaho and is frequently found in the search for other gems. Because it fractures easily with a distinct conchoidal fracture, it was invaluable to primitive man. From it he fashioned tools, weapons, and ornaments. Two forms of obsidian are of special interest. Small spherical drops, transparent and black, are called Apache tears. These are tumbled for baroque jewelry and occasionally faceted. Having a similar form, but frequently in larger spheres, are tektites. Because they are usually entirely unrelated in composition to the country rock where they are found, their origin has been the subject of much scientific debate. The generally accepted theory is that they are of cosmic origin and have fallen from the sky. Collectors seek them because of this interesting theory.

A few other varieties of obsidian having interesting color and displaying attractive phenomena are fashioned into gem stones. Desirable cabochons are cut from black obsidian having white included crystals of feldspar. The included crystals resemble snowflakes and the variety is appropriately called snowflake obsidian.

Transparent material of any color having straight or curved bandings or patterns resulting from double flows is occasionally cut. Red obsidian with black inclusions, sometimes known as mountain mahogany, is also fashioned into cabochons if the material is judged to have sufficient beauty.

Some black obsidian containing included impurities will display either a silver or golden sheen if cut at the correct angle. Still other black obsidian containing minute cracks due to internal strain is iridescent at certain angles of observation and is called rainbow obsidian.

Because of its softness, obsidian polishes with difficulty and loses polish quickly. Occasional pieces do have beauty, justifying their consideration as gem material.

RHODONITE

Rhodonite is normally some shade of red, the red shade turning to black on altering the mineral's manganese content by oxidation. It always occurs in compact massive form, has a vitreous luster, and is hard enough to take and retain a good polish.

The best rhodonite in Idaho comes from a locality in the foothills a few miles south of New Meadows in Adams County (see Field Trip 2). It is an attractive pink with seams of black oxides of manganese. Dendrites are fewer than those in California rhodonite, but its rose pink color is distinctly better. It is also more opaque than the dark red from Broken Hill, Australia. The fine texture and compactness of the Idaho

Courtesy Glen and Ruth Evans

Rhodonite sphere and rough material

material, which has few undesirable colorations, yields beautiful finished cabochons.

SILLIMANITE

Sillimanite, an aluminum silicate mineral, is sometimes called fibrolite because of its fibrous structure. Strong color in sillimanite is very rare. Its usual colors are pale olive green and grayish shades of blue, yellow, brown, or white. Transparent crystals, generally a pale blue, facet beautifully.

In Idaho, sillimanite ranges in size from water-worn pebbles of a few ounces to boulders of several pounds, and is found on the shores and gravel bars of the Clearwater River above Lewiston and on the Salmon River below the town of Salmon. One of the favorite hunting localities is the Big Eddy of the Clearwater above Spaulding. Because recognition of the water-worn pieces is difficult unless the fibrous structure is detected, every inch of the shoreline between low and high water levels should be searched carefully and gravel bars thoroughly combed. Material visible in shallow water should also be observed carefully. Frequently, identity in water is revealed by a sheen from the mineral's fibrous structure.

All the material found in Idaho is opaque and cut cabochon. Some finished stones display interesting color patterns, and all have an appealing pearly luster because of the fibrous structure. A few, containing fibers in a parallel structure, have an attractive chatoyancy.

SPINEL

Spinel, recognized as a gemstone of exceptional beauty, occurs in a wide variety of colors and a wide range of tones and shades within those colors. It is hard enough to take and retain a good polish and to wear as a ring stone. It is produced synthetically in large quantities and sold under various trade names for practically every colored gemstone. In spite of the popularity of the synthetic, the desire for natural spinel continues, and many lovers of fine gems wear natural spinel stones with pride.

The dark green to black variety of spinel, sometimes called ceylonite, occurs in a few places in Idaho. It has been reported as occurring in the contact copper deposits of the Seven Devils district of Adams County. At the head of Wildhorse Canyon, on the east side of Mt. Hyndman in Custer County, is another occurrence of ceylonite. It was found near a lake in a cirque in a crystalline limestone that had undergone a regional metamorphism. The isotropic crystals there are small and a dark bottle green. They are simple octahedrons, the usual habit of spinel.

The same ceylonite variety occurs in abundance as crystal fragments or water-worn pebbles in the gem gravels of Rocky Flat, between McCall and Meadows in Adams and Valley Counties (see Field Trip 2). Most of the specimens are small but can be cut into stones of a few carats. Ceylonite's tone is so dark that only careful observation prevents its being discarded as a worthless piece of non-gem black rock. Its high specific gravity, however, causes it to remain associated with concentrates of other heavy minerals after washing. The beautiful emerald-green of the material is revealed in transmitted light, disclosing its identity. This desirable color can best be secured in a finished stone by facet-cutting a thin stone or fashioning a shallow cabochon.

Because spinel occurs in contact metamorphic and gneissic rocks, both types common in many parts of Idaho, future discoveries of spinel of gem consequence are probable.

STAUROLITE

The term staurolite is derived from two Greek words, *staros,* meaning *cross,* and *lithos,* meaning *stone.* Sometimes it is designated as cross-stone, fairy-stone, or twin-stone. The crystals are prismatic and twinning is frequent. Sometimes interpenetrating twins form the cross that is of gemological interest.

Staurolite occurs in metamorphic rocks; however, it is sometimes recovered from alluvial deposits. It is opaque and ranges from brown almost to black. Deep reddish-brown is most desired. The interpenetrating twins forming a natural cross are prized as curios. The stone is never cut, although sometimes it is polished. In its natural form it is mounted as a pendant, particularly for rosaries, and worn as an amulet for protection against evil.

Finds of staurolite have been reported from two places in

Idaho. In Benewah County about five miles up Carpenter Creek from its junction with the St. Maries River, an extensive ledge of mica schist occurs. The ledge lies from the northeast to the southwest and outcrops where it is cut by a forest road and the creek (see Field Trip 1). Staurolite crystals occur in abundance in the schist, some an inch to an inch-and-one-half in length. Many of them are twinned, and a few of the twin crystals are interpenetrated at right angles forming a natural cross.

Excellently formed crosses have also been found in the southern part of the St. Joe Basin and along the St. Joe-Clearwater divide of Shoshone County. Staurolite is strikingly developed in some of the metamorphosed rocks of the Belt series in this area. Crystals, either twinned and cruciform or simple, well developed prisms, are plentiful in the bluish slate of the upper Wallace formation. Many brown cruciform twins have been recovered from a locality about one-half mile northwest of the summit of Bathtub Mountain, where staurolite occurs in association with kyanite and small pink garnets.

THULITE

The rose-red zoisite, thulite, occurs near Elk River in Clearwater County. It is generally pink but occasionally variegated pink and green. It occurs in granular masses and is always opaque. The patience of the cutter can result in a pleasing cabochon with a good polish.

TOURMALINE

Chemically, tourmaline is exceptionally complex. Variations of the proportions of the many minerals that may be present in its composition cause variations in the color of the mineral. Thus, it may be colorless, red to red-purple, light to dark violet-blue, yellowish-green to bluish-green, brown, or black. Sometimes tourmaline also occurs in parti-colored crystals, usually part light green and part pink, much like the colors of a watermelon. Crystals may be green or yellow on the inside and red on the outside; others are red at one end and green at the other.

A few tourmaline stones fashioned cabochon are chatoyant, usually exhibiting a floating girasol luminescence. Occasionally a narrow chatoyant band occurs, however, and the stone is properly called tourmaline cat's-eye. Some tourmalines also display an alexandrite-like color change. In daylight they are yellowish- to brownish-green; in artificial light, orange-red.

In addition to its intrinsic color beauty and interesting optical properties, tourmaline is hard and tough enough that gemstones fashioned from it are durable, beautiful, and valuable.

All tourmaline so far found in Idaho is of the opaque, black, iron-bearing variety, schorlite. In Blaine County such iron tourmaline occurs in imperfect crystals in the talus at the head of a cirque on the south flank of Mt. Hyndman. Similar but smaller crystals, greenish to brownish-black with a silky luster, occur in the Lava Creek district about twenty miles west of Arco. In Boise County black and bluish-gray tourmaline has been discovered in abundance in large, well formed crystals. Similar but smaller crystals are found associated with corundum in the placer concentrates at Pierce in Clearwater County. In Gem County's High Valley, northeast of Ola, large, well formed, black tourmaline crystals occur in a pegmatite of quartz and feldspar. Although the pegmatite runs for some distance through the valley, outcroppings are concealed by heavy brush and are difficult to find; nevertheless, the area has been highly productive. In Latah County, black tourmaline occurs abundantly in rough crystals in the schists adjacent to the pegmatite masses mined for mica and beryllium near Avon. In Lemhi County, in some of the ores of the Blackbird district, tourmaline occurs as small, rough, black to greenish-black crystals in quartz. In Shoshone County, black tourmaline occurs as fine grains in sedimentary rocks of the Coeur d'Alene district. In a number of places in the Avery district in the southern part of the County, larger crystals occur, some almost an inch in length. In Washington County, one-half mile northwest of the site of the old town of Mineral, small black tourmaline crystals occur in a vein with pyrite, chalcopyrite, and quartz.

Although black tourmaline has comparatively little gem value, it does have interest as a collector's item. Most of the material is friable and difficult to work, but cabochons or faceted stones with a brilliant polish and metallic luster can be fashioned as a reward for effort and patience. Because the mineral occurs so frequently in Idaho, it is probable that more desirable varieties in color and transparency may be found.

VIVIANITE

Vivianite, a hydrous iron phosphate, occurs as single crystals and in clusters. Although it is fragile and soft, and cleaves and fractures easily, its clear, greenish-blue crystals do have gem interest. Frequently vivianite forms on the bones of such extinct animals as the mammoth.

As in the case of apatite, the best gem vivianite comes from the Blackbird district of Lemhi County. However, isolated finds have been reported from Clearwater County. Broad, blue plates of vivianite have been discovered in the Dixie district of Idaho County. Clusters of small crystals of vivianite have also been recovered from the Silver City district of Owyhee County. These crystals have a special interest inasmuch as they are a dark green in transmitted light and azure blue in reflected light.

ZIRCON

Since ancient times zircon has been recognized as a gem mineral. Fine zircons are gems of great beauty. A stone faceted from colorless material rivals the brilliancy of a diamond. It also occurs in many beautiful colors—yellow, orange, red, brown, and blue.

The occurrence of zircon is widely distributed throughout Idaho as a constituent of heavy sands concentrated from gold placer and monozite washings. Like monozite and garnet, much of the zircon is probably derived from the disintegration of, or small pegmatites in, granite. Generally zircon is found as clear, colorless (but sometimes colored), invariably beautiful, sharp, and brilliant crystals of good gem quality, but far too small for gem fashioning. However, its abundance makes it probable that someday someone will discover a locality where conditions have been right for the growth of crystals of gem size.

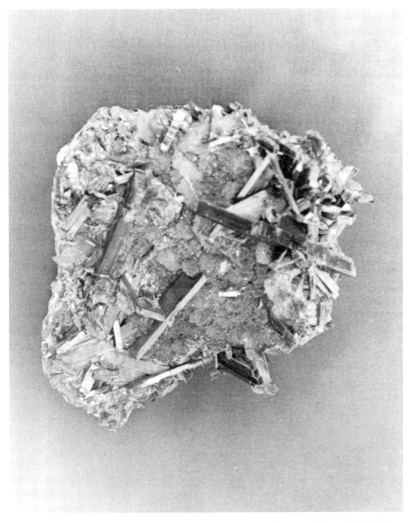

Courtesy Glen and Ruth Evans

Vivianite from Cobalt mines near Cobalt, Idaho

FIELD TRIPS

THE FOLLOWING is not a set of field trips in the strictest sense but a breakdown of Idaho into areas. Within those areas the gem hunter will find spotted for him the various mineral occurrences discussed in this book. Satisfactory coverage of most of the areas would require several days to a week. Shorter trips should be limited to districts within the areas.

FIELD TRIP 1

The world-famous garnet deposits of Latah County, particularly those on Emerald Creek, are visited by thousands of rockhounds each year. To control digging, areas are now leased by the Bureau of Land Management to individuals, and a nominal digging fee is charged. Digging tools and screens are necessary. A well equipped National Forest Camp is available at Emerald Creek, and the area can be reached during all but the severe months of the winter. The beryl-mica mine north of Deary has not been active for some time, and the last few miles of the road are poorly maintained and passable only during summer months. Because a long hike is necessary to reach the Purdue Creek deposit, prior knowledge of whether digging is possible and under what conditions should be ascertained from members of the Moscow Star Garnet Club, Moscow, Idaho, and from inquiry in Bovill.

FIELD TRIP I

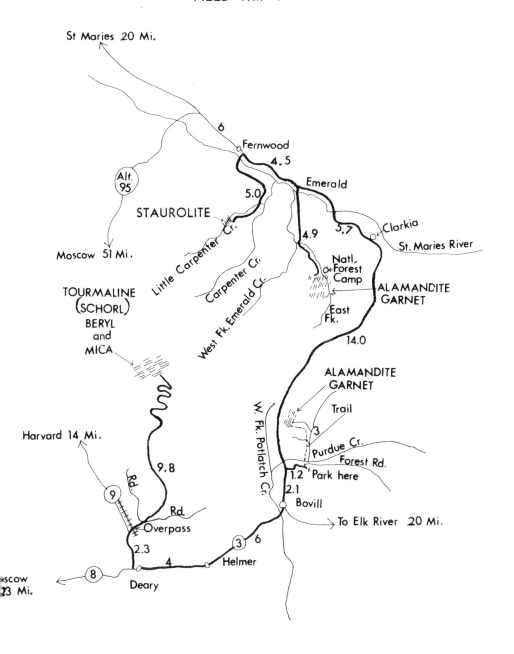

FIELD TRIP 2

The Rocky Flat area, a few miles northwest of McCall, has been much worked, but it is still possible to recover small rolled pebbles of crystal quartz, spinel, and broken pieces of corundum. The corundum in the Burgdorf-Ruby Meadows areas is much more plentiful, but much less of it is of gem quality. In addition to digging tools, a screen is necessary at both locations. Although roads are good, winters are severe, and this is distinctly a summer hunting trip. A good established camp ground with a hot spring is available near Burgdorf.

FIELD TRIP 2

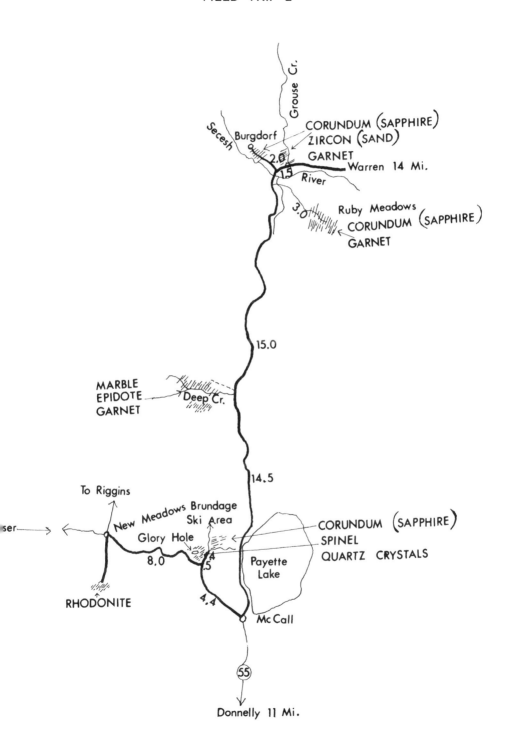

FIELD TRIP 3

Even though the crystal area near Cascade is easily accessible during all but the snowy months of winter, it is still producing quartz crystals, mostly smoky, of excellent quality. The area is tree-covered and brushy. Very few crystals are now available on the surface; most are excavated from small pegmatites in the granite.

The area near Donnelly is difficult to map, as logging roads run in many directions. Even though the crystal area was once mined commercially, the road is now dim and concealed by brush. Travel northwest until an area, scarred by old and recent diggings and cluttered with old pieces of machinery, is reached. The town of Donnelly and the surrounding valley can be seen from the site. Digging tools are necessary, and the trip should be made only during summer months and with a truck or four-wheel drive vehicle.

FIELD TRIP 3

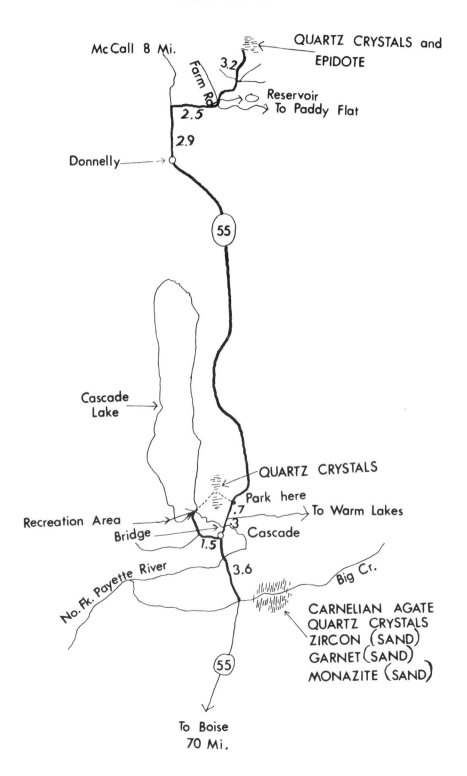

FIELD TRIP 4

This is distinctly a summer trip to a beautiful high mountain country, nearly eight-thousand feet. Roads are sometimes blocked by snow until mid-summer. A few crystals can still be found on the surface, but digging is generally necessary. Camping is possible near the Swamp, when permitted. There is a good established camp with excellent spring water a few miles above the gem area on the road to Trinity Lakes. As the camp is used mostly by game hunters, rock hunters have it to themselves during the summer.

FIELD TRIP 4

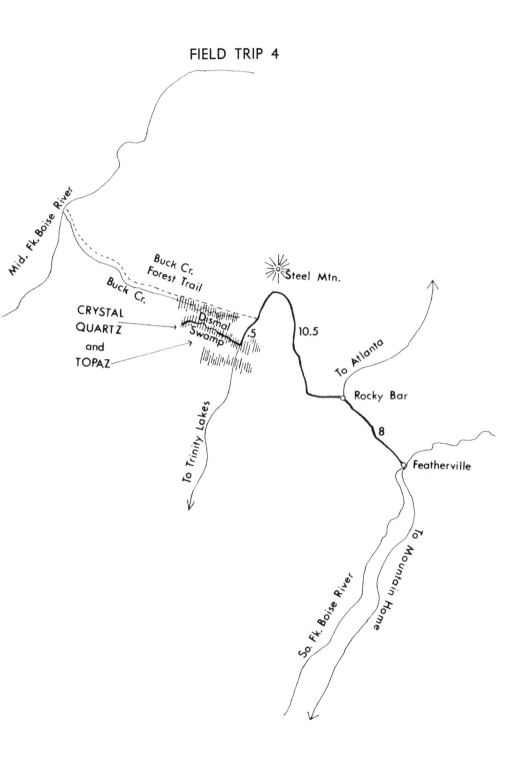

FIELD TRIP 5

The Beacon Hill thunder eggs are highly desirable, and the locality has been worked extensively for many years. Although the eggs were once plentiful and widely scattered, very few can now be found on the surface. Recovery now requires digging with heavy tools. The five-and-one-half miles of the road up the hill is poorly maintained and passable only during summer months. There is no established camp at the diggings and no water. The agate on Hog Creek is scattered over a large area and can be hunted or dug. The petrified wood on Mann and Sage Creeks is no longer plentiful, but of good quality and color (mostly red on Sage Creek). The hillsides should be hunted as well as the creek beds. Established camp grounds are available at the State Park on Mann Creek and at the junction of Mann and Fourth of July Creeks. The area on Sage Creek can be approached from lower down near Midvale, but the Rest Area provides better parking and a shorter hike. In either case a full day is required for satisfactory results.

FIELD TRIP 5

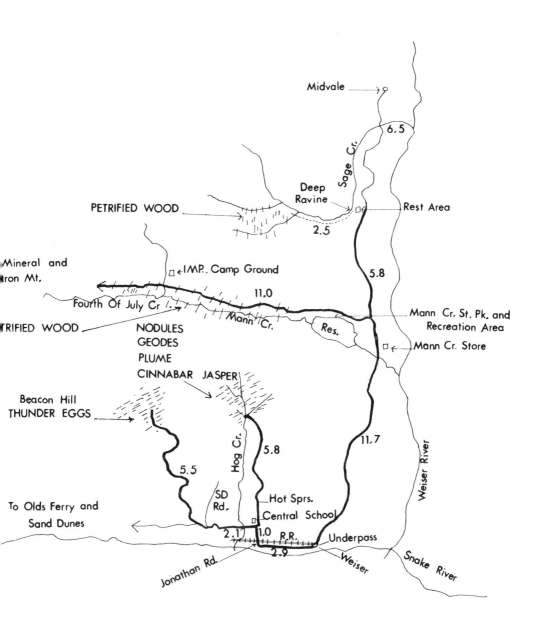

FIELD TRIP 6

Even though this area is only a half-hour drive from Boise, it is still highly productive of quality material. The mine near Rocky Canyon is sometimes closed to the public. The small creeks and gullies are open to both digging and hunting.

FIELD TRIP 6

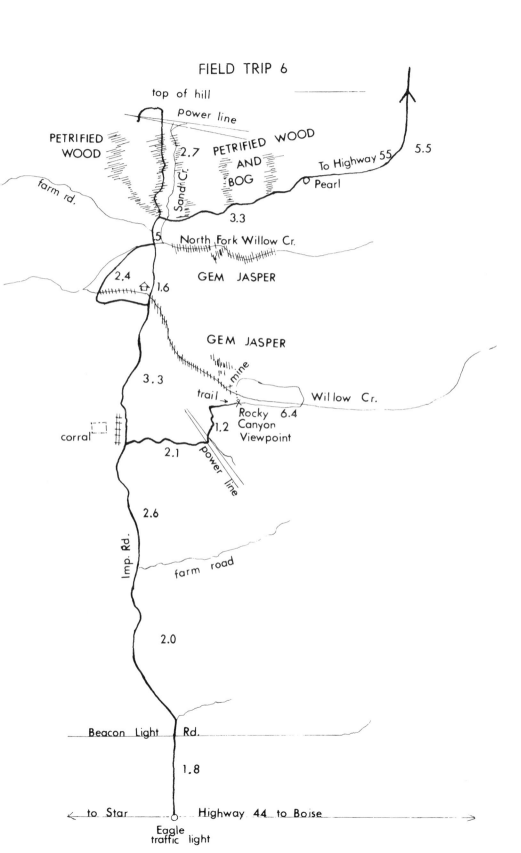

FIELD TRIP 7

Although this area, partly in Idaho and partly in Oregon, has been popular with rock hounds for many years, it is still productive of a variety of material of excellent quality. A trip of several days is necessary for satisfactory results. Roads to the east of the canal are not maintained, but travel on the desert roads is possible most of the year. No water is available and there are no established camp sites. Although some material can still be picked up on the surface, digging is generally necessary and heavy digging tools are recommended.

FIELD TRIP 7

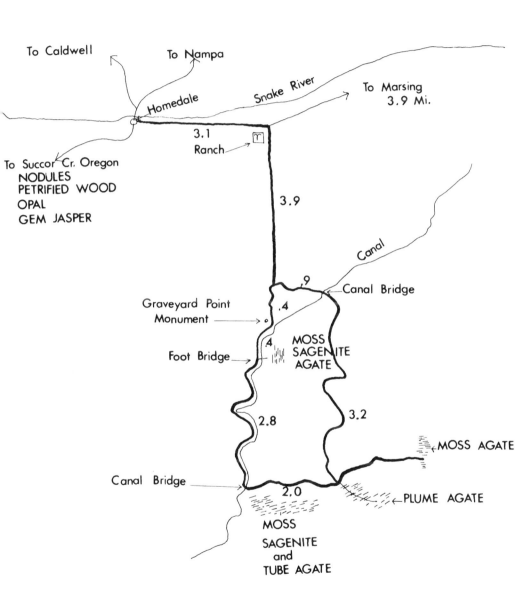

FIELD TRIP 8

This trip, covering a large area and offering a variety of material, requires several days for satisfactory exploration. There are no established camp sites, and little drinking water is available. The spectacular canyons of Poison, Jump, and Squaw Creeks should be viewed and photographed. Digging at the fire opal mine on Squaw Creek is restricted to members of the Idaho Gem Club, Boise, Idaho, and to others having permission of a club officer. Small pieces of the gem jasper, locally called queenstone, can still be picked up on the surface. The petrified wood of the McBride Creek Basin, scattered over a large area, is also usually recovered by searching the surface. In general, however, digging with heavy tools is necessary. Highway 95 is paved and except for a few rock-hound side roads, travel is possible most of the year.

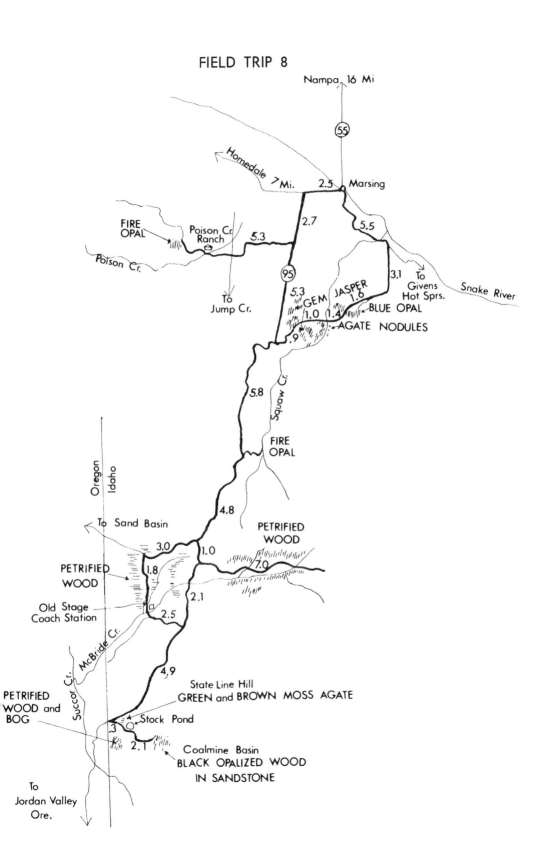

FIELD TRIP 8

Nampa 16 Mi

55

Homedale 7 Mi.

2.5 Marsing

2.7

5.5

FIRE OPAL

Poison Cr. Ranch

5.3

Poison Cr.

95

To Jump Cr.

5.3

3.1 To Givens Hot Sprs.

Snake River

GEM JASPER

1.6

1.0 1.4 BLUE OPAL

.9 AGATE NODULES

Squaw Cr.

5.8

FIRE OPAL

4.8

Oregon | Idaho

To Sand Basin

3.0

PETRIFIED WOOD

1.0

PETRIFIED WOOD

1.8

7.0

Old Stage Coach Station

2.1

2.5

Succor Cr.

McBride Cr.

4.9

State Line Hill
GREEN and BROWN MOSS AGATE

PETRIFIED WOOD and BOG

.3 Stock Pond

2.1 Coalmine Basin
BLACK OPALIZED WOOD
IN SANDSTONE

To Jordan Valley Ore.

FIELD TRIP 9

The petrified wood south of Bruneau, perfectly preserved, is calcified, and much of it is too soft for gem fashioning. Occasional petrified conifer cones are also found. The amethystine agate near the Indian Bathtub is no longer plentiful, but even the recovery of a small amount is rewarding. The Bruneau jasper requires a difficult trip in to a wild desert country. Four-wheel drive vehicles can be driven down the old Indian trail to the bottom of the canyon and the jasper. Most hunters camp at the canyon rim and hike down and up the trail. Highway 51 is paved; other roads are good to passable most of the year. There are no established camps and very little water suitable for drinking; heavy digging tools are necessary at all locations.

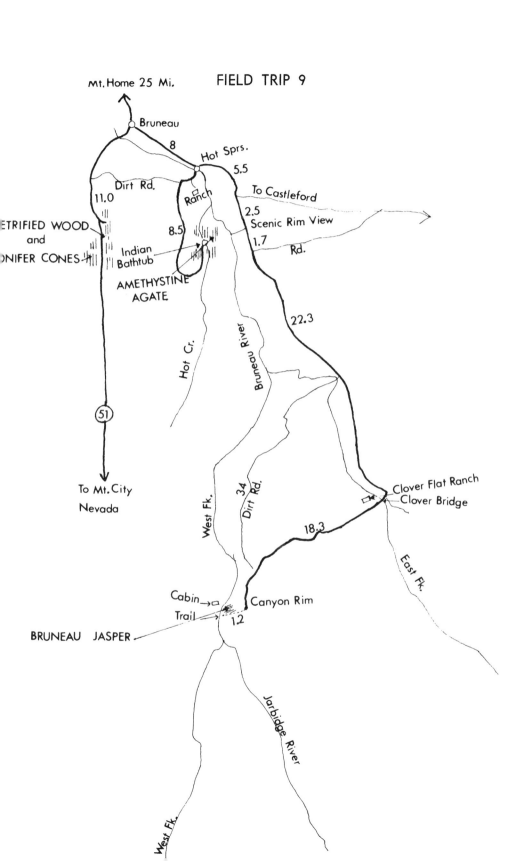

FIELD TRIP 9

FIELD TRIP 10

This is a fascinating trip to an old mining area and is of special interest to mineral collectors. The approach from Sheaville, Oregon, is easier and provides more places for the recovery of a variety of materials. The roads to this high, rugged country are usually rough and passable only during summer months. Water is available but not gasoline, and there are no established camps. The cassiterite is difficult to recover as the rolled pebbles are of such high specific gravity that they quickly work their way to bedrock. Most quartz crystals are recovered from old mine dumps, but many can still be found scattered on the hillsides.

FIELD TRIP 10

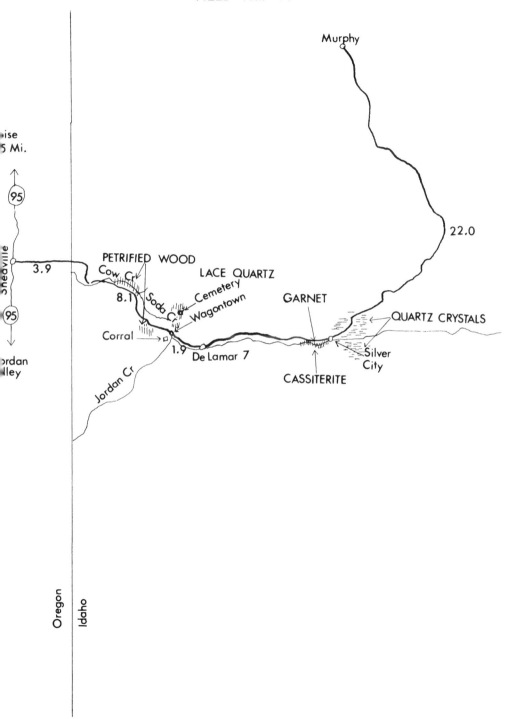

FIELD TRIP 11

The highly mineralized area of South Mountain is a must trip for mineral collectors. On the old mine dumps and in digging areas are the associated minerals of lead, zinc, copper, silver, and iron. Two additional rare minerals that are abundant here are hedenbergite and ilvaite. The mineral lodes occur in calcareous rocks, mostly white marble with dark bandings.

This is a summer trip to a high country on a good but little traveled road. Juniper, pine, and other evergreens cover the hillsides, and willows line the small creeks where many excellent natural camp sites are available. For up-to-date information Everett Jones of the Jordan Valley Gift Shop should be visited.

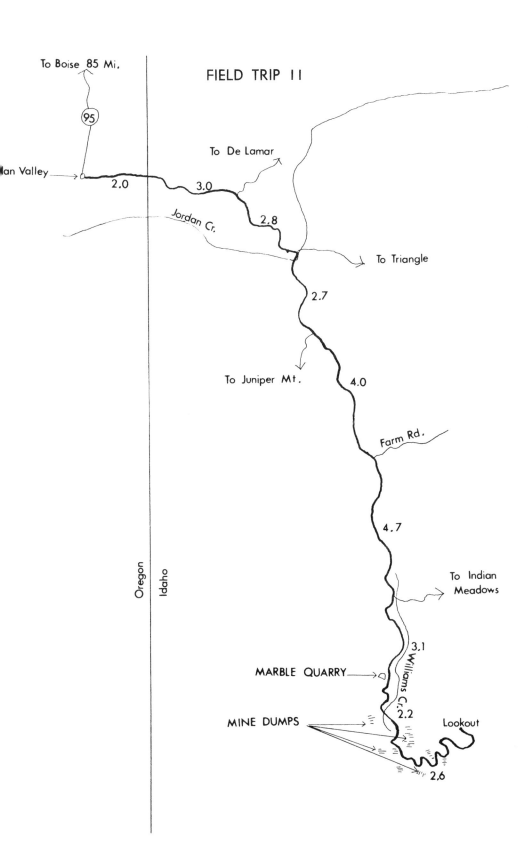

To Boise 85 Mi.

(95)

FIELD TRIP 11

To De Lamar

lan Valley

2.0   3.0

2.8

Jordan Cr.

To Triangle

2.7

To Juniper Mt.   4.0

Farm Rd.

4.7

Oregon   Idaho

To Indian
Meadows

3.1

MARBLE QUARRY

Williams Cr.

2.2

MINE DUMPS

Lookout

2.6

FIELD TRIP 12

The valley of the Little Wood River provides an extensive area open for collecting from early spring to late fall. Although clear agate without interesting character is scattered throughout the area, recovery of desirable agate requires several days of walking and careful searching. Finds are possible on the alluvial fans and in the draws near the road, especially in the early spring. As summer advances, it is necessary to hunt higher and higher in the draws and on the ridges. Only limited recovery is made by digging.

In the draws, just before the road ascends the divide to Bellevue, more green agate occurs, and finds of geodes lined with amethyst crystals have been reported.

The road over the Bellevue divide is generally not open in the early spring; other roads in the area are good. The campground at the Little Wood River Reservoir is large and partially improved. Ample parking space is available at the sheep corral above Muldoon, but there are no camping facilities.

FIELD TRIP 12

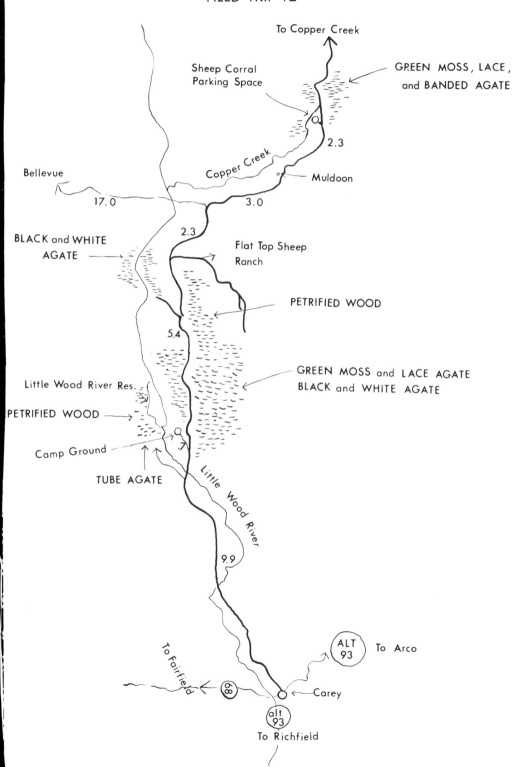

FIELD TRIP 13

The Hammond Canyon area northwest of Arco can be approached from Alternate 93 about four miles southwest of Arco, but is more easily found by the route shown. After reaching the fork of the Newman Canyon road to the right, the Hammond Canyon road crosses a flat that is usually very dusty in the summer. This is a cattle-raising area, and numerous gates must be passed through. Roads are not marked, and from the Newman Canyon junction the road is unimproved. There are no good camping places.

The most desirable material is tube agate; however, there are a few nodules and some green and red jasper. Broken pieces of agate are scattered over the area, and many chips and an occasional arrowhead are evidence that Indians visited the location. Recovery of desirable agate requires walking slowly and searching the sagebrush-covered flats and hillsides.

The recovery of nodules from the Lime and Wet Creek areas demands much walking on rather steep hillsides. A few geodes lined with amethyst crystals may be found.

The drive on a good gravel road through the spectacular and beautiful Pass Creek Gorge is worth the trip if no nodules are found. Many undeveloped but naturally attractive camping places are available.

If one does not desire to double back, he can drive on down the unspoiled Pahsimeroi Valley to Patterson, May, and the Salmon River, exploring for promising new locations. The majestic mountains of the Lost River and Lemhi Ranges, the mile-high valleys, many clear streams, groves of aspen and scattered fir trees, with an almost sure sighting of deer and antelope, make this a rewarding summer trip.

FIELD TRIP 13

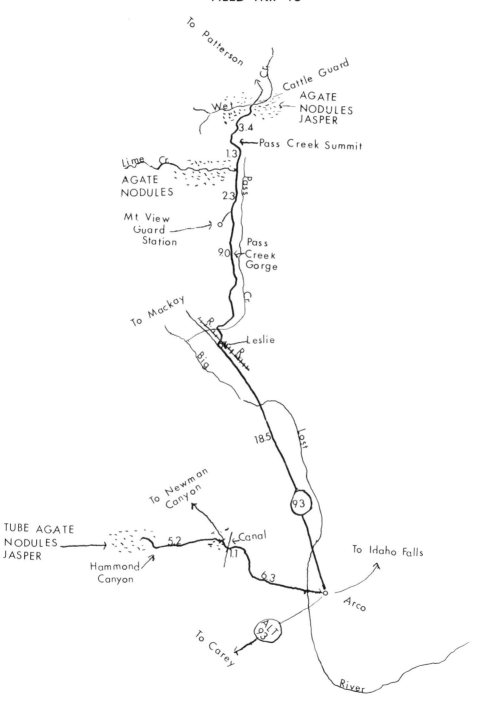

FIELD TRIP 14

Although this large area of many locations, usually referred to as the Challis area, has been hunted extensively, it continues to produce high quality material.

Broken pieces of agate are scattered beside the road at the top of Grand View Canyon, but reaching the collecting area necessitates a climb up a steep ravine or on the hillside around it. No campground is available at the site.

The Lime Gulch location is accessible by a sandy and rocky road up Lime Creek and by Jeep trails up Devil's Canyon and Hole-in-Rock Creek. Collecting here is possible all during the year; however, some winter days, with snow piled deep in the surrounding mountains, can be uncomfortably cold, while midsummer days are frequently very hot. Some material is recovered by digging in the banks of dry washes, but hunting the draws, alluvial fans, and hillsides continues to be the most profitable method. Much of the petrified wood is too soft for gem use, but some brownish-red, orange, and green pieces are hard and well silicified. Unimproved campgrounds are available along Lime Creek.

The locations on the East Fork of the Salmon River, particularly Road Creek, have been popular summer collecting areas for a long time but are still productive. It is an area of much natural beauty with occasional views of the White Cloud peaks in the background. There are no improved campgrounds at any of the East Fork locations, but several are available within a short drive.

At most of the locations on the East Fork, the agate occurs in a volcanic red rock formation. A few nodules and some seam agate are recovered from the solid rock with the aid of points and a crack hammer, but most is picked up loose on talus slopes and alluvial fans. Red and blue nodules with interesting fortification bandings are the most desirable material, while a rare find of a geode lined with amethyst crystals continues to be the prize.

FIELD TRIP 14

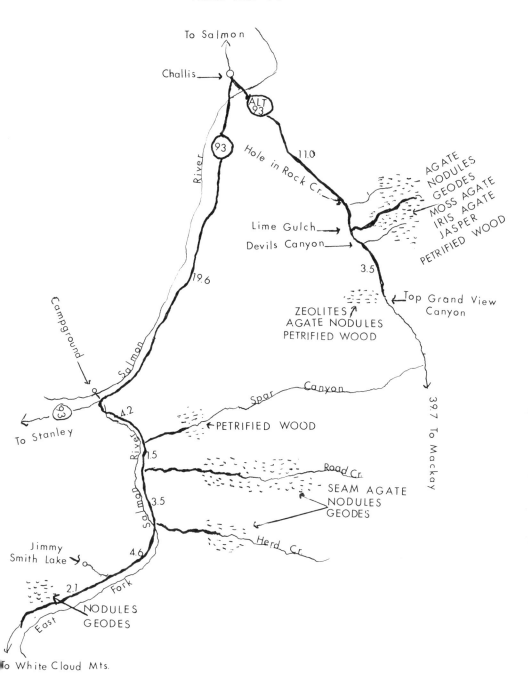

To Salmon

Challis

ALT 93

93

Hole in Rock Cr.

11.0

River

AGATE
NODULES
GEODES
MOSS AGATE
IRIS AGATE
JASPER
PETRIFIED WOOD

Lime Gulch

Devils Canyon

3.5

19.6

Top Grand View
Canyon

Campground

ZEOLITES
AGATE NODULES
PETRIFIED WOOD

Salmon

39.7 To Mackay

Spar   Canyon

63

4.2

To Stanley

PETRIFIED WOOD

River

1.5

Road Cr.

Salmon

3.5

SEAM AGATE
NODULES
GEODES

Herd Cr.

Jimmy
Smith Lake

4.6

Fork

2.1

NODULES
GEODES

East

To White Cloud Mts.

INDEX